Joshua through Malachi & Ancient Greece

Second Edition

A Year of Lesson Plans
for History, Geography, and Bible
(Grades 1–12)

by
Sonya Shafer

Joshua through Malachi and Ancient Greece, Second Edition

ISBN 978-1-61634-241-8 printed
ISBN 978-1-61634-242-5 electronic download

Cover Design: John Shafer

Published by
Simply Charlotte Mason, LLC
930 New Hope Road #11-892
Lawrenceville, Georgia 30045
simplycharlottemason.com

Printed by PrintLogic, Inc.
Monroe, Georgia, USA

Contents

How to Use

This book of lesson plans contains book suggestions and assignments for every grade level, so you can combine all of your students into one family study.

- The **Family** instructions are for everyone to do together.
- Additional **Grade Level** assignments are given for students to complete either independently or with the parent. Your choice.
- **Optional** hands-on activities are also listed. Feel free to skip them, substitute different ones, or add more.

Complete one lesson per day to finish this study in a school year. The lesson plans in this book follow this five-day schedule.

Day 1	Day 2	Day 3	Day 4	Day 5
Bible	Bible and Geography	Bible	History	History

You will find lots of helpful information and Internet links on the Links and Tips page for this book at http://simplycm.com/joshua-links

Complete Year's Book List

Family (all students)

- Bible
- *Material World* **and** *Hungry Planet: What the World Eats* by Peter Menzel
  These two wonderful living geography books are used with our *Visits to...* books every year in all the grades.
- *The Story of the Greeks* by H. A. Guerber, edited by Christine Miller, Fourth edition (Nothing New Press edition)
  A living narrative that weaves the story of Ancient Greece. This edited version removes evolutionary comments and honors the Biblical accounts.
- *The Stuff They Left Behind: From the Days of Ancient Greece* portfolio
  A collection of large full-color photographs of artifacts with leading thoughts and discussion questions.
- *Then and Now Bible Maps* from Rose Publishing
  An excellent geography resource used in three of our six history studies.
- *Visits to the Middle East* notebook by Sonya Shafer (one for each student)
  Each *Visits to...* book guides your student to spend time exploring a continent or region through map work, living books, and the personal photographs and living travelogue contained in *Material World* and *Hungry Planet: What the World Eats*. Ideas are also included for additional activities.

plus...

Grades 1–3

- *Our Little Athenian Cousin of Long Ago* by Julia Darrow Cowles
- *Our Little Spartan Cousin of Long Ago* by Julia Darrow Cowles
  Both of these great books introduce young students to daily life in Ancient Greece through a storyline of a young person who lived there.

Grades 4–6

- *Archimedes and the Door of Science* by Jeanne Bendick
- *Herodotus and the Road to History* by Jeanne Bendick
  These two living biographies are a wonderful introduction to a scientist and historian of Ancient Greece.
- *Our Little Athenian Cousin of Long Ago* by Julia Darrow Cowles (if desired)
- *Our Little Spartan Cousin of Long Ago* by Julia Darrow Cowles (if desired)
  Students in grades 4–6 may also find interesting the two "cousin" books recommended for grades 1–3.

Grades 7–9

- *Black Ships Before Troy* by Rosemary Sutcliff
  A narrative of the Trojan War by a master storyteller.
- Book of Centuries (one for each student)
- *Discovering Doctrine* by Sonya Shafer (one for each student)
  A multi-year project for observing, recording, and organizing Biblical truths as the student reads through the Bible.
- *The Parthenon* by Elizabeth Mann
  This short, beautifully illustrated book gives a nice overview of Ancient Greece and the role of the Parthenon.
- *The Wanderings of Odysseus* by Rosemary Sutcliff
  A narrative of the Odyssey by a master storyteller.
- *Wisdom for Life: A Proverbs Bible Study* by Sonya Shafer (one for each student)
  Students read through the book of Proverbs several times, focusing on what it says about a variety of topics.
- *A Young Macedonian in the Army of Alexander the Great* by Alfred Church
  A wonderful historical fiction that brings to life some of the details of life and battle in the time of Ancient Greece, as well as how the various countries and their citizens interacted with each other.

Grades 10–12

- Book of Centuries (one for each student)
- *Discovering Doctrine* by Sonya Shafer (one for each student)
  A multi-year project for observing, recording, and organizing Biblical truths as the student reads through the Bible.
- *The Odyssey* by Homer
  Literature from Ancient Greece translated into English. This epic poem recounts the fanciful and adventurous journey home from the Trojan War by one of the Greek warriors, Odysseus.
- *Plutarch's Lives,* biography of Alexander, by Plutarch
  A biography of Alexander the Great written by a man who lived soon after.
- *The Trial and Death of Socrates* by Plato
  Written by Socrates' pupil, Plato, this work examines the events through dialogue.
- *A Victor of Salamis* by William Stearns Davis
  A historical fiction written in the late 1800s that makes the political and cultural aspects of Ancient Greece and Persia come alive.
- *Wisdom for Life: A Proverbs Bible Study* by Sonya Shafer (one for each student)
  Students read through the book of Proverbs several times, focusing on what it says about a variety of topics.

Optional Book List

- *The Big Picture Bible Time Line* by Carol Eide (grades 1–6)
  If you want a time line for the younger children while the older children add entries to their Books of Centuries, the pages in this book will be a great help. The drawings and captions are simple and will help the children remember the people and events of Joshua through Malachi in order. Ancient Greece events are not included in this time line, but could easily be added if desired.
  An easy way to store these pictures as the timeline grows is to tape them end to end and wrap them around a dowel rod, making the timeline into a scroll. It saves a lot of space, and students can still unroll the scroll to various places and look at the events in chronological order. Note: Some dates may not be identical to the ones listed in the Book of Centuries column in this book. But you can still follow the captions to note when to use the pictures.
- *The Child's Story Bible* by Catherine Vos (grades 1–3)
  Recommended for portions of the Old Testament account that might best be reworded to be appropriate for younger children. (See Living Books explanation on page 120.)

Other Materials

- Small sheet of poster board and felt-tip markers (for Judges diagram, optional)
- Self-stick notes
- Sheet of poster board and felt-tip markers (for Kings chart, optional)
- Various materials for hands-on projects (optional)

Suggestions for
Where to Find the Books

Simply Charlotte Mason

- Book of Centuries (one for each student in grades 7–12)
- *Discovering Doctrine* by Sonya Shafer (one for each student in grades 7–12)
- *Hungry Planet* by Peter Menzel (Family)
- *Material World* by Peter Menzel (Family)
- *The Stuff They Left Behind: From the Days of Ancient Greece* portfolio (Family)
- *Visits to the Middle East* notebook by Sonya Shafer (one for each student in the Family)
- *Wisdom for Life: A Proverbs Bible Study* by Sonya Shafer (one for each student in grades 7–12)

Public Domain

(You can probably download these for free at http://gutenberg.org, http://books.google.com, or http://archive.org.)

- *The Odyssey* by Homer (grades 10–12)
- *Our Little Athenian Cousin of Long Ago* by Julia Darrow Cowles (grades 1–3 or 1–6)
- *Our Little Spartan Cousin of Long Ago* by Julia Darrow Cowles (grades 1–3 or 1–6)
- *Plutarch's Lives,* biography of Alexander, by Plutarch (grades 10–12)
- *The Trial and Death of Socrates* by Plato (grades 10–12)
- *A Victor of Salamis* by William Stearns Davis (grades 10–12)
- *A Young Macedonian in the Army of Alexander the Great* by Alfred Church (grades 7–9)

Your Local Library

(These are the titles that a library is most likely to have. You might also check for the titles listed under Your Favorite Book Store. If your library does not have access to a book listed here, add it to your Book Store list.)

- *Archimedes and the Door of Science* by Jeanne Bendick (grades 4–6)
- *Herodotus and the Road to History* by Jeanne Bendick (grades 4–6)
- *The Parthenon* by Elizabeth Mann (grades 7–9)

Your Favorite Book Store

(Check http://amazon.com, http://christianbook.com, http://rainbowresource.com, or other favorite book sources.)

- *The Big Picture Bible Time Line* by Carol Eide (optional for grades 1–6)
- *Black Ships Before Troy* by Rosemary Sutcliff (grades 7–9)
- *The Child's Story Bible* by Catherine Vos (optional for grades 1–3)
- *The Story of the Greeks* by H. A. Guerber, edited by Christine Miller, Fourth edition (Nothing New Press edition; for Family)
- *Then and Now Bible Maps* from Rose Publishing (Family)
- *The Wanderings of Odysseus* by Rosemary Sutcliff (grades 7–9)

Visit http://simplycm.com/joshua-links for helpful links to the books.

Term 1

(12 weeks; 5 lessons/week)

Term 1 Book List

Family

- Bible
- *Material World* **and** *Hungry Planet: What the World Eats* by Peter Menzel
- *The Story of the Greeks* by H. A. Guerber, edited by Christine Miller
- *The Stuff They Left Behind: From the Days of Ancient Greece* portfolio
- *Then and Now Bible Maps* from Rose Publishing
- *Visits to the Middle East* notebook by Sonya Shafer (one for each student)

Plus . . .

Grades 1–3

- *Our Little Spartan Cousin of Long Ago* by Julia Darrow Cowles

Grades 4–6

- *Herodutus and the Road to History* by Jeanne Bendick
- *Our Little Spartan Cousin of Long Ago* by Julia Darrow Cowles (if desired)

Grades 7–9

- *Black Ships Before Troy* by Rosemary Sutcliff
- Book of Centuries (one for each student)
- *Discovering Doctrine* by Sonya Shafer (one for each student)
- *The Parthenon* by Elizabeth Mann
- *Wisdom for Life: A Proverbs Bible Study* by Sonya Shafer (one for each student)

Grades 10–12

- Book of Centuries (one for each student)
- *Discovering Doctrine* by Sonya Shafer (one for each student)
- *The Odyssey* by Homer
- *Wisdom for Life: A Proverbs Bible Study* by Sonya Shafer (one for each student)

Optional

- *The Big Picture Bible Time Line* by Carol Eide (grades 1–6)
- Self-stick notes
- Small sheet of poster board and felt-tip markers (for Judges diagram)
- Various materials for hands-on projects

What You Will Cover As a Family

Bible: *Joshua—1 Samuel*

Geography: *Middle East, with special emphasis on Israel and Turkey*

History: *Ancient Greece, from the first inhabitants through Draco and Solon*

Term 1 At a Glance

	Family	Grades 1-3	Grades 4-6	Grades 7-9	Grades 10-12
Week 1, Lessons 1-5					
Bible	Joshua			Proverbs Study	Proverbs Study
History	Story of the Greeks, ch. 1-4	Our Little Spartan Cousin, ch. 1	Herodotus, Preface and ch. 1	The Parthenon	The Odyssey, bk. 1, 2
Geography	Visits to the Middle East, Visit 1				
Week 2, Lessons 6-10					
Bible	Joshua			Proverbs Study	Proverbs Study
History	Story of the Greeks, ch. 5-8	Our Little Spartan Cousin, ch. 2	Herodotus, ch. 2	Black Ships Before Troy, ch. 1, 2	The Odyssey, bk. 3, 4
Geography	Visits to the Middle East, Visit 2				
Week 3, Lessons 11-15					
Bible	Joshua			Proverbs Study	Proverbs Study
History	Story of the Greeks, ch. 9-12	Our Little Spartan Cousin, ch. 3	Herodotus, ch. 3	Black Ships Before Troy, ch. 3, 4	The Odyssey, bk. 5, 6
Geography	Visits to the Middle East, Visit 3				
Week 4, Lessons 16-20					
Bible	Judges			Proverbs Study	Proverbs Study
History	Story of the Greeks, ch. 13-15	Our Little Spartan Cousin, ch. 4	Herodotus, ch. 4	Black Ships Before Troy, ch. 5, 6	The Odyssey, bk. 7, 8
Geography	Visits to the Middle East, Visit 4				
Week 5, Lessons 21-25					
Bible	Judges; Ruth			Proverbs Study	Proverbs Study
History	Story of the Greeks, ch. 16-19	Our Little Spartan Cousin, ch. 5	Herodotus, ch. 5	Black Ships Before Troy, ch. 7, 8	The Odyssey, bk. 9, 10
Geography	Visits to the Middle East, Visit 5				
Week 6, Lessons 26-30					
Bible	Ruth; Judges			Proverbs Study	Proverbs Study
History	Story of the Greeks, ch. 20-23	Our Little Spartan Cousin, ch. 6	Herodotus, ch. 6	Black Ships Before Troy, ch. 9, 10	The Odyssey, bk. 11, 12
Geography	Visits to the Middle East, Visit 6				

Use this chart to see what your family and each of your students will be studying week by week during this term. You will also be able to see when each book is scheduled to be used.

	Family	Grades 1–3	Grades 4–6	Grades 7–9	Grades 10–12
Week 7, Lessons 31–35					
Bible	Judges; 1 Samuel			Proverbs Study	Proverbs Study
History	Story of the Greeks, ch. 24–26	Our Little Spartan Cousin, ch. 7	Herodotus, ch. 7	Black Ships Before Troy, ch. 11, 12	The Odyssey, bk. 13, 14
Geography	Visits to the Middle East, Visit 7				
Week 8, Lessons 36–40					
Bible	1 Samuel			Proverbs Study	Proverbs Study
History	Story of the Greeks, ch. 27–29	Our Little Spartan Cousin, ch. 8	Herodotus, ch. 8	Black Ships Before Troy, ch. 13, 14	The Odyssey, bk. 15, 16
Geography	Visits to the Middle East, Visit 8				
Week 9, Lessons 41–45					
Bible	1 Samuel			Proverbs Study	Proverbs Study
History	Story of the Greeks, ch. 30–33	Our Little Spartan Cousin, ch. 9	Herodotus, ch. 9	Black Ships Before Troy, ch. 15, 16	The Odyssey, bk. 17, 18
Geography	Visits to the Middle East, Visit 9				
Week 10, Lessons 46–50					
Bible	1 Samuel			Proverbs Study	Proverbs Study
History	Story of the Greeks, ch. 34–36	Our Little Spartan Cousin, ch. 10	Catch Up	Black Ships Before Troy, ch. 17, 18	The Odyssey, bk. 19, 20
Geography	Visits to the Middle East, Visit 10				
Week 11, Lessons 51–55					
Bible	1 Samuel			Proverbs Study	Proverbs Study
History	Story of the Greeks, ch. 37, 38	Our Little Spartan Cousin, ch. 11		Black Ships Before Troy, ch. 19	The Odyssey, bk. 21, 22
Geography	Visits to the Middle East, Visit 11				
Week 12, Lessons 56–60					
Bible	Exam or Catch Up			Proverbs Study	Proverbs Study
History	Exam or Catch Up or Project				The Odyssey, bk. 23, 24
Geography	Visits to the Middle East, Visit 12				

Lesson 1: Joshua Takes Command

Materials Needed

- Bible
- *The Stuff They Left Behind: From the Days of Ancient Greece*
- *Wisdom for Life* (grades 7–12)
- *Discovering Doctrine* (grades 7–12)

Family: Write on a sheet of paper or small white board the words "The Ten Plagues," "Egypt," "The Ten Commandments," "Moses," and "Wilderness." Ask students what they remember about those events, places, and person. Review with students how before Moses died, God told him to appoint Joshua as the next leader of the Israelites—the one who would lead them into the Promised Land. Read together Joshua 1 and 2 and ask for an oral narration.

> ***Tip:*** *For younger children, you may want to break up the reading into two or more shorter sections and ask for a narration for each section.*

Display the Hittite Bas Relief Sculpture picture from *The Stuff They Left Behind: From the Days of Ancient Greece.* Use the Leading Thoughts to discuss it.

Grades 7–12: Students in grades 7–12 have two ongoing Bible projects throughout this year. First, they should be reading one chapter of Proverbs every day and recording their findings on their selected topic in *Wisdom for Life.* See the *Wisdom for Life* book for details.

> ***Tip:*** *If students read a Proverbs chapter every day, seven days a week, they will read through the book of Proverbs eight times during the school year and complete all eight topics listed in* Wisdom for Life; *if they read chapters only five days a week, they will complete six of the topics from the Bible study. Work with your student to determine the best pace for him or her. Remember, the goal is that your student gains wisdom from God's Word; the pace is secondary. You will see reminders throughout these lesson plans to accommodate both paces.*

Second, they should be looking for any doctrinal truths in the passages read. Joshua 1 contains some wonderful truths about God and the Bible that students in grades 7–12 could record in their *Discovering Doctrine* books.

Lesson 2: Crossing the Jordan & Visit 1 to the Middle East

Materials Needed

- Bible
- *Visits to the Middle East*

Book of Centuries Timeline

Book of Centuries Timeline

- *Wisdom for Life* (grades 7–12)
- *Discovering Doctrine* (grades 7–12)

Family: Ask students what they recall from last time's reading about God's encouragements to the Israelites as they prepared to enter the Promised Land.

Tip: You don't need to require another full narration in this preparatory stage. You simply want them to recall that event so they can mentally connect today's reading to it.

Explain that there was still one obstacle between Israel and the Promised Land: the flooded Jordan River. Read together Joshua 3 and 4 and ask for an oral narration.

Tip: Explain that the events of the Old Testament took place in the Middle East for the most part. You will be studying that region this year both in Israel's day and in modern day.

Family: Complete Visit 1 in *Visits to the Middle East.*

Grades 7–12: Continue working on *Wisdom for Life* Proverbs study and watching for truths to record in *Discovering Doctrine.*

Tip: Did your older students notice the descriptive name for God given in Joshua 3:13? That truth should go in their Discovering Doctrine *notebooks.*

Lesson 3: The Fall of Jericho

Materials Needed

- Bible
- *Then and Now Bible Maps*
- *Wisdom for Life* (grades 7–12)
- *Discovering Doctrine* (grades 7–12)

Joshua conquers Jericho (c. 1451 B.C.)

Family: Ask students what they recall from last time's reading about Israel's crossing the Jordan River. Explain that today's reading will be about the first famous battle in the Promised Land. Display map 9, Holy Land - Old Testament, in *Then and Now Bible Maps*. Locate Mount Nebo, where Moses died, then move directly west to cross the Jordan River and see which town the Israelites would encounter first. (Jericho.)

Read together Joshua 5 and 6 and ask for an oral narration.

Tip: For younger children, you may want to start the reading at Joshua 5:10.

Grades 7–12: Continue working on *Wisdom for Life* Proverbs study and watching for truths to record in *Discovering Doctrine.*

Book of Centuries Timeline

Lesson 4: The First Inhabitants of Greece

Materials Needed

- *The Story of the Greeks*
- *Then and Now Bible Maps*
- *Herodotus and the Road to History* (grades 4–6)
- *The Parthenon* (grades 7–9)
- *The Odyssey* (grades 10–12)

Family: Explain that while you will be studying what happened as the Israelites settled into their Promised Land, you will also be reading about another people group who lived across the Mediterranean Sea. Read together *The Story of the Greeks*, chapters 1 and 2, "The Beginning of the Nations" and "The First Inhabitants of Greece." As you read chapter 2, display map 15 in *Then and Now Bible Maps* and help students locate Egypt, Phoenicia, Greece, and the islands near it. Ask for an oral narration.

Tower of Babel dispersion (c. 2242 B.C.)

***Tip:** The short chapters in* The Story of the Greeks *provide natural breaks if you would prefer to read and narrate in two shorter portions rather than one longer portion. Simply stop and ask for a narration at the end of each chapter.*

Grades 4–6: Read together or assign as independent reading *Herodotus and the Road to History*, Preface and chapter 1, " I Am Herodotus." Ask for an oral or written narration.

Grades 7–9: Read together or assign as independent reading the first half of *The Parthenon* and ask for an oral or written narration.

Grades 10–12: Read together or assign as independent reading *The Odyssey,* book 1, and ask for an oral or written narration.

***Reminder:** Get* Black Ships Before Troy *for lesson 9 for grades 7–9.*

Lesson 5: Old Greek Fairy Tales

Materials Needed

- *The Story of the Greeks*
- *Our Little Spartan Cousin of Long Ago* (grades 1–3 or 1–6)
- *The Parthenon* (grades 7–9)
- *The Odyssey* (grades 10–12)

Book of Centuries Timeline

Family: Ask students what they recall from last time's reading about the first inhabitants of Greece. Explain that the Greeks were well-known for the myths they told. In today's reading students will discover how those myths came about. Read together *The Story of the Greeks*, chapters 3 and 4, "Old Greek Fairy Tales" and "More Greek Fairy Tales." Ask for an oral narration.

Grades 1–3 or 1–6: Read together *Our Little Spartan Cousin of Long Ago*, chapter 1, "A Spartan Company."

***Tip:** Students in grades 4–6 may also listen to* Our Little Spartan Cousin *readings if desired.*

Grades 7–9: Read together or assign as independent reading the last half of *The Parthenon* and ask for an oral or written narration.

***Tip:** Narrations can be done in many ways. Visit our website at http://simplycm.com/narration-ideas for many more creative ideas that encourage students to narrate.*

Grades 10–12: Read together or assign as independent reading *The Odyssey*, book 2, and ask for an oral or written narration.

Lesson 6: Achan and Ai

Materials Needed

- Bible
- *Wisdom for Life* (grades 7–12)
- *Discovering Doctrine* (grades 7–12)

Family: Ask students what they recall from last time's reading about the battle of Jericho. Explain that in today's reading, you will learn how one man's disobedience affected the next battle. Write the names "Achan" and "Ai" on a small white board or sheet of paper large enough for all the students to see. Tell them how to pronounce the words and that this man and this city played key roles in the account today. Read together Joshua 7 and 8 and ask for an oral narration.

Grades 7–12: Continue working on *Wisdom for Life* Proverbs study and watching for truths to record in *Discovering Doctrine*.

Lesson 7: The Gibeonites' Deception & Visit 2 to the Middle East

Materials Needed

- Bible

- *Visits to the Middle East*
- *Material World*
- *Wisdom for Life* (grades 7–12)
- *Discovering Doctrine* (grades 7–12)

Family: Ask students what they recall from last time's reading about Achan and the battle at Ai. Explain that when some of the enemies in the land saw how the Israelites were winning the battles, they decided to take a different approach and see if they could trick the Israelites. Read together Joshua 9 and ask for an oral narration.

Family: Complete Visit 2 in *Visits to the Middle East.*

Grades 7–12: Continue working on *Wisdom for Life* Proverbs study and watching for truths to record in *Discovering Doctrine.*

Lesson 8: Southern and Northern Campaigns

Materials Needed

- Bible
- *Wisdom for Life* (grades 7–12)
- *Discovering Doctrine* (grades 7–12)

Family: Ask students what they recall from last time's reading about the Gibeonites' deception. Explain that Joshua did battle with the other cities and God helped him gain the victories in miraculous ways sometimes. Read together Joshua 10 and 11 and ask for an oral narration.

Grades 7–12: Continue working on *Wisdom for Life* Proverbs study and watching for truths to record in *Discovering Doctrine.*

Tip: From this point on, the plans will not specifically mention Discovering Doctrine *in every lesson but will periodically remind you to make sure older children are up to date with their* Discovering Doctrine *notebooks and their Book of Centuries entries.*

Lesson 9: The Founding of Many Important Cities

Materials Needed

- *The Story of the Greeks*

Book of Centuries Timeline

Book of Centuries Timeline

Cecrops founds the city of Athens (1556 B.C.)

- *Herodotus and the Road to History* (grades 4–6)
- *Black Ships Before Troy* (grades 7–9)
- *The Odyssey* (grades 10–12)

Family: Ask students what they recall from last time's reading about Greek fairy tales, or myths. Write the word "Athens" on a sheet of paper or small white board and display it for students to see. Explain that this became one of the greatest cities in Greece. People were living in it about 100 years before Joshua led the Israelites into Canaan, and it still exists today.

Read together *The Story of the Greeks*, chapters 5 and 6, "The Founding of Many Important Cities" and "Perseus and Mycenae." Locate Attica and Athens, Boeotia, Argolis, and the Isthmus of Corinth on the map of Ancient Greece on page 15 in *The Story of the Greeks* as they are mentioned. Ask for an oral narration.

Grades 4–6: Read together or assign as independent reading *Herodotus and the Road to History*, chapter 2, " I Grow Up." Ask for an oral or written narration.

Grades 7–9: Read together or assign as independent reading *Black Ships Before Troy,* chapter 1, "The Golden Apple," and ask for an oral or written narration.

Grades 10–12: Read together or assign as independent reading *The Odyssey,* book 3, and ask for an oral or written narration.

Lesson 10: The Sons of Deucalion

Materials Needed

- *The Story of the Greeks*
- *(optional) Then and Now Bible Maps*
- *Our Little Spartan Cousin of Long Ago* (grades 1–3 or 1–6)
- *Black Ships Before Troy* (grades 7–9)
- *The Odyssey* (grades 10–12)

Family: Ask students what they recall about the towns of Greece and the story of Perseus. Write the words "Deucalion, Daedalus, Icarus" on a sheet of paper or small white board for students to see. Ask if they recall who Deucalion was. Explain that the tale of Daedalus and Icarus is a well-known one and they should listen carefully so they will be able to retell it well. Read together *The Story of the Greeks*, chapters 7 and 8, "The Sons of Deucalion" and "Daedalus and Icarus." Locate Thessaly and Thermopylae on the map of Ancient Greece on page 15 in *The Story of the Greeks* as they are mentioned. When Crete is mentioned you can find it on either the map on page 16 or in *Then and Now Bible Maps,* map 15, to show its proximity to Greece. Ask for an oral narration.

Tip: *Allow the students to look at the key words you posted while they narrate. Those key words will help them stay focused and organize their thoughts. It will also be good training for them to listen for key words* *themselves, eventually, when none might be pointed out ahead of time.*

Grades 1–3 or 1–6: Read together *Our Little Spartan Cousin of Long Ago,* chapter 2, "The Assembly."

Grades 7–9: Read together or assign as independent reading *Black Ships Before Troy,* chapter 2, "Ship-Gathering," and ask for an oral or written narration.

Grades 10–12: Read together or assign as independent reading *The Odyssey,* book 4, and ask for an oral or written narration.

***Tip:** Make sure older children are up to date with their* Discovering Doctrine *notebooks and their Book of Centuries entries.*

Lesson 11: The Land Divided Between the Tribes

Materials Needed

- Bible
- *Then and Now Bible Maps*
- *Wisdom for Life* (grades 7–12)

Family: Ask students what they recall from last time's reading about Joshua's victories in the Promised Land. Explain that the Israelites had effectively cut the country in half. Now they could split the land into segments and assign one of the twelve tribes to each segment, trusting them to complete the conquest and drive out the enemies in their territories. Read together Joshua 13:1–6. Explain that Joshua 13—19 details how the land was divided between the tribes. Look at map 9, Holy Land - Old Testament, in *Then and Now Bible Maps,* using the color key to see where each tribe settled.

Ask students what they recall about a certain man named Caleb, who had stood with Joshua as a spy many years ago. Explain that God had kept him alive during the years of wandering, while all the others of his and Joshua's generation had died, and Caleb was still strong in the Lord. Read together Joshua 14:6–15 and ask for an oral narration. Then read Joshua 19:49–51 to discover Joshua's inheritance of land.

Grades 7–12: Continue working on *Wisdom for Life* Proverbs study.

Lesson 12: Cities of Refuge & Visit 3 to the Middle East

Materials Needed

- Bible

Book of Centuries Timeline

Book of Centuries Timeline

- *Then and Now Bible Maps*
- *Visits to the Middle East*
- *Wisdom for Life* (grades 7–12)

Family: Ask students what they recall from last time's reading about the twelve tribes' land assignments. Explain that now the tribes needed to put into place some of God's specific plans for living in the Promised Land. The Lord had already given these instructions to Moses; now Joshua was being careful to carry them out. Read together Joshua 20. As each of the six tribes is mentioned, in whose territory a city of refuge would be, locate its place on map 9, Holy Land - Old Testament, in *Then and Now Bible Maps*. Notice how the cities were spread out on both sides of the Jordan to make them within reach of all the people.

***Tip:** Those students who have completed the* Jashub's Journal *Bible study (recommended in the Genesis through Deuteronomy & Ancient Egypt lesson plans) may be able to contribute more details about the cities of refuge. If your older students have not completed that Bible study, now would be a fitting time to include it if desired.*

Read together Joshua 21:43–45 and chapter 22 and ask for an oral narration.

Family: Complete Visit 3 in *Visits to the Middle East*.

Grades 7–12: Continue working on *Wisdom for Life* Proverbs study.

Lesson 13: Joshua's Final Challenge

Materials Needed

- Bible
- *Wisdom for Life* (grades 7–12)

Family: Ask students what they recall from last time's reading about the situation that almost started a civil war between the tribes on the west side of Jordan and those on the east side. Explain that Joshua was now growing old and knew he would die soon. Ask students what they would say to the twelve tribes as a final word if they had been Joshua. Read together Joshua 23 and 24 and ask for an oral narration.

Grades 7–12: Continue working on *Wisdom for Life* Proverbs study.

***Tip:** Joshua 24 contains some truths about God for the* Discovering Doctrine *notebook.*

Lesson 14: The Adventures of Jason

Book of Centuries Timeline

Materials Needed
- *The Story of the Greeks*
- *The Stuff They Left Behind: From the Days of Ancient Greece*
- *Herodotus and the Road to History* (grades 4–6)
- *Black Ships Before Troy* (grades 7–9)
- *The Odyssey* (grades 10–12)

Family: Ask students what they recall from last time's reading about the Hellenes and the tale of Daedalus and Icarus. Look carefully at the map on page 15 in *The Story of the Greeks*, Ancient Greece, and find the area labeled Peloponnesus. (Look in the lower left section, just off the coast.) Read together *The Story of the Greeks*, chapter 9, "The Adventures of Jason."

Display and discuss the picture of the Jason and the Snake Cup from *The Stuff They Left Behind: From the Days of Ancient Greece.*

Then read together *The Story of the Greeks*, chapter 10, "Theseus visits the Labyrinth." Ask for an oral narration.

Grades 4–6: Read together or assign as independent reading *Herodotus and the Road to History*, chapter 3, "My Travels Begin." Ask for an oral or written narration.

Grades 7–9: Read together or assign as independent reading *Black Ships Before Troy,* chapter 3, "Quarrel with the High King," and ask for an oral or written narration.

Grades 10–12: Read together or assign as independent reading *The Odyssey,* book 5, and ask for an oral or written narration.

Lesson 15: The Terrible Prophecy

Materials Needed
- *The Story of the Greeks*
- *Our Little Spartan Cousin of Long Ago* (grades 1–3 or 1–6)
- *Black Ships Before Troy* (grades 7–9)
- *The Odyssey* (grades 10–12)

Family: Ask students what they recall from last time's reading about the heroes of Ancient Greece: Jason and Theseus in the Labyrinth. Explain that today students will learn the answer to an ancient riddle: What creature walks on four feet in the morning, two at noon, and three at night? Allow students to guess if desired, then tell them the answer is in the story of Oedipus. Write that name on a sheet of paper or small white board for students to see how it is spelled. Read together *The Story of the Greeks*, chapters 11 and 12, "The Terrible Prophecy" and "The Sphinx's Riddle." Ask for an oral narration.

Book of Centuries Timeline

Grades 1–3 or 1–6: Read together *Our Little Spartan Cousin of Long Ago,* chapter 3, "Foraging."

Grades 7–9: Read together or assign as independent reading *Black Ships Before Troy,* chapter 4, "Single Combat," and ask for an oral or written narration.

Grades 10–12: Read together or assign as independent reading *The Odyssey,* book 6, and ask for an oral or written narration.

***Tip:** Make sure older children are up to date with their* Discovering Doctrine *notebooks and their Book of Centuries entries.*

 Lesson 16: The Sin Cycle in Judges

Materials Needed

- Bible
- *Then and Now Bible Maps*
- Sheet of paper or poster board; felt-tip marker
- *Wisdom for Life* (grades 7–12)

Family: Ask students what they recall from last time's reading of Joshua's final words to the twelve tribes of Israel. Review on map 9, Holy Land - Old Testament, in *Then and Now Bible Maps* where each tribe settled. Ask students what the main assignment was for those tribes. Explain that in today's reading you will find out whether each tribe completed its assignment to drive out the enemies. Read together Judges 1 and note which tribes failed to drive out the former inhabitants and idol worshipers.

Explain that the students will see similar actions repeated throughout the book of Judges. Give students a sheet of paper or poster board and a felt-tip marker. Read together Judges 2 and have the students create and label a Sin Cycle diagram like the one below, using their own words to describe each step in the cycle (outlined in verses 11–19). (Example: Step 1–worshiped other gods; Step 2–attacked by enemy; Step 3–called out to God; Step 4–God delivered.) Post their Sin Cycle diagram where students can see it during the next few weeks as you study the book of Judges.

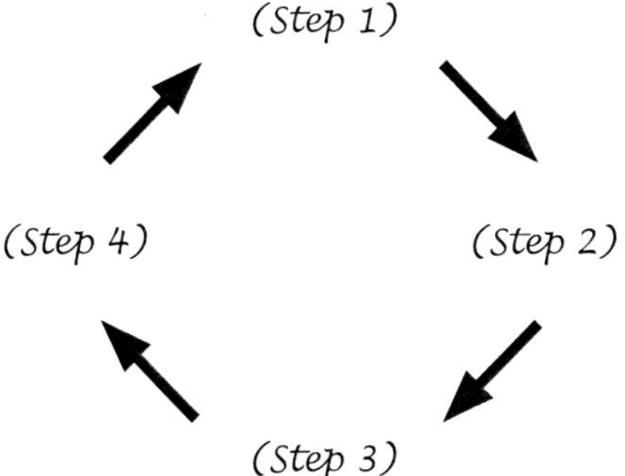

Grades 7–12: Continue working on *Wisdom for Life* Proverbs study.

Book of Centuries Timeline

Lesson 17: Othniel, Ehud, and Shamgar & Visit 4 to the Middle East

Materials Needed

- Bible
- Small self-stick notes
- *Then and Now Bible Maps*
- *Visits to the Middle East*
- *Wisdom for Life* (grades 7–12)

Family: Ask students what they recall about the Israelites' actions after Joshua died. Read together Judges 3 and ask the students to find an object around the house that reminds them of each judge: Othniel, Ehud, Shamgar. Ask them to explain why the objects they selected fit each judge. (Example: a knife for Ehud; a stick for Shamgar.)

Othniel called by God to deliver and judge Israel (1405 B.C.)

Turn to map 9, Holy Land - Old Testament, in *Then and Now Bible Maps*. Make a small sticky-note label for each judge and attach it to the map near the location of each judge's battle. (Remember, Othniel was Caleb's son-in-law and Caleb's family settled near Hebron. See Joshua 14:13–15 and 15:13–17.)

Ehud delivers Israel (1325 B.C.)

Tip: It's easy for us to think that the battles and judges involved all of Israel. This map exercise will help students realize how the judges and battles were localized in various segments of the land.

Family: Complete Visit 4 in *Visits to the Middle East.*

Grades 7–12: Continue working on *Wisdom for Life* Proverbs study.

Lesson 18: Deborah

Materials Needed

- Bible
- Small self-stick notes
- *Then and Now Bible Maps*
- *Wisdom for Life* (grades 7–12)

Family: Ask students what they recall about the judges of whom they read last time: Othniel, Ehud, and Shamgar. Review the Sin Cycle diagram that the students created in lesson 16. Read together Judges 4 and 5. Ask the students to find an object around the house that reminds them of the account of Deborah and to explain their selection. Make a small sticky-note

Deborah judges Israel (1285 B.C.)

Book of Centuries Timeline

label for Deborah and attach it to map 9 in *Then and Now Bible Maps* near the location of this enemy.

Grades 7–12: Continue working on *Wisdom for Life* Proverbs study.

Lesson 19: Blindness and Death of Oedipus

Materials Needed

- *The Story of the Greeks*
- *Herodotus and the Road to History* (grades 4–6)
- *Black Ships Before Troy* (grades 7–9)
- *The Odyssey* (grades 10–12)

Oedipus marries his mother and reigns in Thebes (1300 B.C.)

Family: Ask students what they recall from last time's reading about Oedipus, the terrible prophecy about him, and the sphinx's riddle. Explain that in today's reading they will hear the rest of Oedipus' story. Read together *The Story of the Greeks*, chapter 13, "Blindness and Death of Oedipus." Ask for an oral narration.

Tip: When you see a Greek name that ends in es, *that final syllable is usually pronounced EEZ. So Eteocles will be pronounced ee-TEE-o-cleez and his brother will be pronounced pol-ih-NIE-seez. (The main exception to this guidelines is the city of Thebes, which is pronounced THEEBZ, as is commonly heard today.) Watch for names that end in* es; *you will see many in this study of Ancient Greece.*

Grades 4–6: Read together or assign as independent reading *Herodotus and the Road to History*, chapter 4, "To the North." Ask for an oral or written narration.

Grades 7–9: Read together or assign as independent reading *Black Ships Before Troy*, chapter 5, "The Women of Troy," and ask for an oral or written narration.

Grades 10–12: Read together or assign as independent reading *The Odyssey*, book 7, and ask for an oral or written narration.

Lesson 20: The Brothers' Quarrel

Materials Needed

- *The Story of the Greeks*
- *Our Little Spartan Cousin of Long Ago* (grades 1–3 or 1–6)
- *Black Ships Before Troy* (grades 7–9)
- *The Odyssey* (grades 10–12)

Book of Centuries Timeline

Family: Ask students what they recall from last time's reading about the end of Oedipus. Write the word "fate" on a sheet of paper or small white board and discuss what it means. Read together *The Story of the Greeks*, chapters 14 and 15, "The Brothers' Quarrel" and "The Taking of Thebes." Ask for an oral narration.

Grades 1–3 or 1–6: Read together *Our Little Spartan Cousin of Long Ago*, chapter 4, "The Public Tables."

Grades 7–9: Read together or assign as independent reading *Black Ships Before Troy,* chapter 6, "The High King's Embassy," and ask for an oral or written narration.

Grades 10–12: Read together or assign as independent reading *The Odyssey,* book 8, and ask for an oral or written narration.

Lesson 21: Gideon

Materials Needed

- Bible
- Small self-stick notes
- *Then and Now Bible Maps*
- *Wisdom for Life* (grades 7–12)

Family: Ask students to retrieve the household items they have selected for the previous readings and tell what they remember about each judge: Othniel, Ehud, Shamgar, Deborah. Write each judge's name on a small white board or sheet of paper for all the students to see how they are spelled. Explain that you are going to read about another judge today. Add "Gideon" to the list.

Gideon delivers Israel (1245 B.C.)

Read together Judges 6 and 7. Ask the students to find an object around the house that reminds them of the account of Gideon and to explain their selection. Make a small sticky-note label for Gideon and attach it to map 9 in *Then and Now Bible Maps* near the location of this battle. (Notice which tribes were involved.)

Grades 7–12: Continue working on *Wisdom for Life* Proverbs study.

Lesson 22: Abimelech & Visit 5 to the Middle East

Materials Needed

- Bible
- *Visits to the Middle East*
- *Wisdom for Life* (grades 7–12)

Book of Centuries Timeline

Family: Add "Abimelech" to your list of judges' names from lesson 21. Read together Judges 8 and 9. Ask the students to find an object around the house that reminds them of the account of Abimelech and to explain their selection.

Family: Complete Visit 5 in *Visits to the Middle East.*

Grades 7–12: Continue working on *Wisdom for Life* Proverbs study.

Lesson 23: Ruth Stays with Naomi

Materials Needed

- Bible
- *Then and Now Bible Maps*
- *Wisdom for Life* (grades 7–12)

Family: Ask students to summarize the time of the judges so far. Explain that the events of Ruth happened during the time of the judges. Read together Ruth 1:1 and locate Moab on map 9, Holy Land - Old Testament, in *Then and Now Bible Maps.* Remind students that one of the first judges, Ehud, had to battle the king of Moab. Read the rest of Ruth 1 and 2 and ask for an oral narration.

Grades 7–12: Continue working on *Wisdom for Life* Proverbs study.

Tip: If your student has been reading Proverbs seven days a week, he should be ready to finish up the first topic and begin a new one this week. Assign a written narration that summarizes his findings if desired.

Lesson 24: The Childhood of Paris

Materials Needed

- *The Story of the Greeks*
- *Then and Now Bible Maps*
- *Herodotus and the Road to History* (grades 4–6)
- *Black Ships Before Troy* (grades 7–9)
- *The Odyssey* (grades 10–12)

Family: On map 15 in *Then and Now Bible Maps* or on the Ancient Greece map on page 15 of *The Story of the Greeks* have students locate Athens and Sparta then look across the Aegean Sea for Troy. Read together *The Story of the Greeks*, chapters 16 and 17, "The Childhood of Paris" and "The Muster of the Troops." Ask for an oral narration.

Grades 4–6: Read together or assign as independent reading *Herodotus and* *the Road to History*, chapter 5, "Back to Samos and Away Again, to Babylon." Ask for an oral or written narration.

Grades 7–9: Read together or assign as independent reading *Black Ships Before Troy*, chapter 7, "The Horses of King Rhesus," and ask for an oral or written narration.

Grades 10–12: Read together or assign as independent reading *The Odyssey*, book 9, and ask for an oral or written narration.

Book of Centuries Timeline

Lesson 25: The Sacrifice of Iphigenia

Materials Needed

- *The Story of the Greeks*
- *Our Little Spartan Cousin of Long Ago* (grades 1–3 or 1–6)
- *Black Ships Before Troy* (grades 7–9)
- *The Odyssey* (grades 10–12)

Family: Ask students what they recall from last time's reading about the events leading up to war against Paris of Troy. Explain that in today's reading they will hear the beginnings of this famous war, the Trojan War. Read together *The Story of the Greeks*, chapters 18 and 19, "The Sacrifice of Iphigenia" and "The Wrath of Achilles." Ask for an oral narration.

Trojan War (1194–1184 B.C.)

Grades 1–3 or 1–6: Read together *Our Little Spartan Cousin of Long Ago*, chapter 5, "Chartas' Home."

Grades 7–9: Read together or assign as independent reading *Black Ships Before Troy*, chapter 8, "Red Rain," and ask for an oral or written narration.

Grades 10–12: Read together or assign as independent reading *The Odyssey*, book 10, and ask for an oral or written narration.

Tip: *Make sure older children are up to date with their* Discovering Doctrine *notebooks and their Book of Centuries entries.*

Lesson 26: The Kinsman Redeemer

Materials Needed

- Bible
- *Wisdom for Life* (grades 7–12)

Family: Ask students what they recall from last time's reading about Ruth.

Book of Centuries Timeline

Explain that you will finish her story today. Read together Ruth 3 and 4 and ask for an oral narration.

Grades 7–12: Continue working on *Wisdom for Life* Proverbs study.

Lesson 27: Samson's Early Years & Visit 6 to the Middle East

Materials Needed

- Bible
- Small self-stick notes
- *The Stuff They Left Behind: From the Days of Ancient Greece*
- *Then and Now Bible Maps*
- *Visits to the Middle East*
- *Wisdom for Life* (grades 7–12)

Family: Display and discuss the picture of the Traditional Enemies Inlays from *The Stuff They Left Behind: From the Days of Ancient Greece.*

Birth of Samson (1155 B.C.)

Explain that the next judge of Israel battled one of those enemies. Read together Judges 13 and 14. Ask the students to find an object around the house that reminds them of this account of Samson and to explain their selection. Make a small sticky-note label for Samson and attach it to map 9 in *Then and Now Bible Maps* near the location of his battles. (Near Philistia.)

Family: Complete Visit 6 in *Visits to the Middle East.*

Grades 7–12: Continue working on *Wisdom for Life* Proverbs study.

Tip: Judges 13 contains some truths about angels that can go in the Discovering Doctrine *notebooks.*

Lesson 28: Samson and Delilah

Materials Needed

- Bible
- *Wisdom for Life* (grades 7–12)

Family: Ask students what they recall from last time's reading about Samson. Remind students, if they did not mention it, that Samson's bride was given to his friend when Samson left. Read together Judges 15 and 16. Ask the students to find an object around the house that reminds them of the end of Samson and to explain their selection.

Grades 7–12: Continue working on *Wisdom for Life* Proverbs study.

Lesson 29: Death of Hector and Achilles

Book of Centuries Timeline

Materials Needed

- *The Story of the Greeks*
- *The Stuff They Left Behind: From the Days of Ancient Greece*
- *Herodotus and the Road to History* (grades 4–6)
- *Black Ships Before Troy* (grades 7–9)
- *The Odyssey* (grades 10–12)

Family: Ask students what they recall from last time's reading about the Trojan War and Achilles' part in it. Explain that in today's reading they will find out how that war ended. Read together *The Story of the Greeks*, chapters 20 and 21, "Death of Hector and Achilles" and "The Burning of Troy." Ask for an oral narration.

Display and discuss the picture of the Ajax and Achilles Jar from *The Stuff They Left Behind: From the Days of Ancient Greece.*

Grades 4–6: Read together or assign as independent reading *Herodotus and the Road to History*, chapter 6, "I Go to Egypt." Ask for an oral or written narration.

Grades 7–9: Read together or assign as independent reading *Black Ships Before Troy*, chapter 9, "Battle for the Ships," and ask for an oral or written narration.

Grades 10–12: Read together or assign as independent reading *The Odyssey*, book 11, and ask for an oral or written narration.

Lesson 30: Heroic Death of Codrus

Materials Needed

- *The Story of the Greeks*
- *Our Little Spartan Cousin of Long Ago* (grades 1–3 or 1–6)
- *Black Ships Before Troy* (grades 7–9)
- *The Odyssey* (grades 10–12)

Family: Display the map of Ancient Greece on page 15 of *The Story of the Greeks.* Have students locate Peloponnesus and ask them what shape they think that peninsula resembles. Have them locate Athens and Sparta. Explain that throughout Greek history there was an ongoing rival between those two cities, and today's reading will explain what started the feud. Read together *The Story of the Greeks*, chapters 22 and 23, "Heroic Death of Codrus" and "The Blind Poet." Ask for an oral narration.

Homer composes the Iliad and the Odyssey (c. 800 B.C.)

Tip: *If you have a student in grades 10–12 who has been reading a translation of Homer's* Odyssey, *ask him or her to tell a little about it when you read the chapter on "The Blind Poet."*

Book of Centuries Timeline

Grades 1–3 or 1–6: Read together *Our Little Spartan Cousin of Long Ago*, chapter 6, "Sparta's Laws."

Grades 7–9: Read together or assign as independent reading *Black Ships Before Troy*, chapter 10, "The Armor of Achilles," and ask for an oral or written narration.

Grades 10–12: Read together or assign as independent reading *The Odyssey*, book 12, and ask for an oral or written narration.

Lesson 31: Micah's Idols

Materials Needed

- Bible
- *Wisdom for Life* (grades 7–12)

Family: Ask students what they recall about Samson. Ask them to describe Samson's character and what that can tell us about the general direction of the Israelite people during this time of the judges.

Explain that the reading today will give them more insight into the spiritual state of the Israelites. Read together Judges 17 and 18 and ask for an oral narration.

Grades 7–12: Continue working on *Wisdom for Life* Proverbs study.

> ***Tip:*** *If your student has been reading Proverbs five days a week, he should be ready to finish up the first topic and begin a new one this week. Assign a written narration that summarizes his findings if desired.*

Lesson 32: Samuel Is Born & Visit 7 to the Middle East

Materials Needed

- Bible
- *Visits to the Middle East*
- Hungry Planet: What the World Eats
- *Wisdom for Life* (grades 7–12)

Samuel is born (c. 1150 B.C.)

Family: Ask students what they recall about the time of the judges. Explain that God was about to raise up a new leader, one who would serve Him well. Some people call this man the final judge and the first prophet. Read together 1 Samuel 1:1—2:11 and ask for an oral narration.

Family: Complete Visit 7 in *Visits to the Middle East.*

Grades 7–12: Continue working on *Wisdom for Life* Proverbs study.

Tip: 1 Samuel 2 contains some truths about God that can go in the Discovering Doctrine *notebooks.*

Book of Centuries Timeline

Lesson 33: Eli's Wicked Sons

Materials Needed

- Bible
- *Wisdom for Life* (grades 7–12)

Family: Ask students what they recall from last time's reading about Hannah and her son Samuel. Remind students that things had not changed in Israel; Samuel was born during the time of the judges. But he chose to follow the Lord no matter what. Read together 1 Samuel 2:12—4:22 and ask for an oral narration.

Grades 7–12: Continue working on *Wisdom for Life* Proverbs study.

Lesson 34: The Rise of Sparta

Materials Needed

- *The Story of the Greeks*
- *Herodotus and the Road to History* (grades 4–6)
- *Black Ships Before Troy* (grades 7–9)
- *The Odyssey* (grades 10–12)

Family: Ask students what they recall about the Heroic Age of Greece. They might retell the story of Jason, Theseus, Oedipus, or Achilles. Remind students that what they will read from here on is actual history based on records that were kept. First they will learn about Sparta.

If you have a student in grades 1–6 who has been reading *Our Little Spartan Cousin of Long Ago*, ask him to tell what he has learned about Sparta so far. Then read together *The Story of the Greeks*, chapters 24 and 25, "The Rise of Sparta" and "The Spartan Training." Ask for an oral narration.

Sparta founded (1490 B.C.)

Grades 4–6: Read together or assign as independent reading *Herodotus and the Road to History*, chapter 7, "I Write My Histories." Ask for an oral or written narration.

Grades 7–9: Read together or assign as independent reading *Black Ships Before Troy*, chapter 11, "Vengeance for Patroclus," and ask for an oral or written narration.

Grades 10–12: Read together or assign as independent reading *The Odyssey*, book 13, and ask for an oral or written narration.

Book of Centuries Timeline

Lesson 35: The Brave Spartan Boy

Materials Needed

- *The Story of the Greeks*
- *Our Little Spartan Cousin of Long Ago* (grades 1–3 or 1–6)
- *Black Ships Before Troy* (grades 7–9)
- *The Odyssey* (grades 10–12)

Family: Ask students what they recall from last time's reading about Sparta and the Spartan way of life. Read together *The Story of the Greeks*, chapter 26, "The Brave Spartan Boy." Ask for an oral narration.

Grades 1–3 or 1–6: Read together *Our Little Spartan Cousin of Long Ago*, chapter 7, "The Festival."

Grades 7–9: Read together or assign as independent reading *Black Ships Before Troy,* chapter 12, "Funeral Games," and ask for an oral or written narration.

Grades 10–12: Read together or assign as independent reading *The Odyssey,* book 14, and ask for an oral or written narration.

Tip: Make sure older children are up to date with their Discovering Doctrine *notebooks and their Book of Centuries entries.*

Lesson 36: The Ark Returns

Materials Needed

- Bible
- *Wisdom for Life* (grades 7–12)

Family: Ask students what they recall from last time's reading about Eli and his wicked sons. If students don't mention it, remind them that the Ark of the Covenant had been stolen by the Philistines. Explain that today's reading will tell them what happened to those who stole it—something that made them want to give it back. Read together 1 Samuel 5—7 and ask for an oral narration.

Grades 7–12: Continue working on *Wisdom for Life* Proverbs study.

Lesson 37: Saul, Israel's First King & Visit 8 to the Middle East

Materials Needed

- Bible

- *Visits to the Middle East*
- *Wisdom for Life* (grades 7–12)

Family: Ask students what they recall from last time's reading about the return of the Ark and the battle against the Philistines. Discuss what effect Samuel's example might have on Israel. What would it take to keep Israel wholly following the Lord God amidst their ungodly neighbors? Explain that the neighbors' influence was great. Read together 1 Samuel 8—10 and ask for an oral narration.

Family: Complete Visit 8 in *Visits to the Middle East.*

Grades 7–12: Continue working on *Wisdom for Life* Proverbs study.

Lesson 38: Saul Confirmed as King

Materials Needed
- Bible
- *Wisdom for Life* (grades 7–12)

Family: Ask students what they recall from last time's reading about how Saul was appointed as king. Explain that in today's reading, Saul took over the leadership in a decisive way. Read together 1 Samuel 11 and 12 and ask for an oral narration.

Grades 7–12: Continue working on *Wisdom for Life* Proverbs study.

Lesson 39: Public Tables in Sparta

Materials Needed
- *The Story of the Greeks*
- *Herodotus and the Road to History* (grades 4–6)
- *Black Ships Before Troy* (grades 7–9)
- *The Odyssey* (grades 10–12)

Family: Ask students what they recall from previous readings about Lycurgus and the baby he saved to become king of Sparta. Read together *The Story of the Greeks*, chapters 27 and 28, "Public Tables in Sparta" and "Laws of Lycurgus." Ask for an oral narration.

Grades 4–6: Read together or assign as independent reading *Herodotus and the Road to History*, chapter 8, "To Athens." Ask for an oral or written narration.

Grades 7–9: Read together or assign as independent reading *Black Ships*

Book of Centuries Timeline

Saul becomes first king of Israel (1095 B.C.)

Laws of Lycurgus established in Sparta (923 B.C.)

Book of Centuries Timeline

Before Troy, chapter 13, "Ransom for Hector," and ask for an oral or written narration.

Grades 10–12: Read together or assign as independent reading *The Odyssey,* book 15, and ask for an oral or written narration.

Lesson 40: The Messenian War

Materials Needed

- *The Story of the Greeks*
- *Our Little Spartan Cousin of Long Ago* (grades 1–3 or 1–6)
- *Black Ships Before Troy* (grades 7–9)
- *The Odyssey* (grades 10–12)

Family: Ask students what they recall from previous readings about Sparta. Discuss what kind of soldiers they think the Spartans would make and why. Read together *The Story of the Greeks*, chapter 29, "The Messenian War." Locate Messenia on the Ancient Greece map on page 15 when it is mentioned. Ask for an oral narration.

Grades 1–3 or 1–6: Read together *Our Little Spartan Cousin of Long Ago*, chapter 8, "Work and Play."

Grades 7–9: Read together or assign as independent reading *Black Ships Before Troy,* chapter 14, "The Luck of Troy," and ask for an oral or written narration.

Grades 10–12: Read together or assign as independent reading *The Odyssey,* book 16, and ask for an oral or written narration.

Lesson 41: Samuel Rebukes Saul

Materials Needed

- Bible
- *Wisdom for Life* (grades 7–12)

Family: Ask students what they recall from last time's reading about Saul's leadership in Israel and Samuel's charge to them both. Explain that Saul had a grown son named Jonathan and that today's reading will tell about some of the battles they fought together. Read together 1 Samuel 13 and 14 and ask for an oral narration.

Grades 7–12: Continue working on *Wisdom for Life* Proverbs study.

Lesson 42: David Anointed as New King & Visit 9 to the Middle East

Materials Needed
- Bible
- *Visits to the Middle East*
- *Wisdom for Life* (grades 7–12)

Family: Ask students what they recall from last time's reading about Saul and Jonathan in battle. Explain that in today's reading, Saul engaged in a battle that changed his whole future. Read together 1 Samuel 15 and 16 and ask for an oral narration.

Family: Complete Visit 9 in *Visits to the Middle East.*

Grades 7–12: Continue working on *Wisdom for Life* Proverbs study.

Tip: 1 Samuel 15 contains some truths about God and about sin that can go in the Discovering Doctrine *notebooks. (Note: No more tips about specific passages that contain truths for the notebooks will be listed in these lesson plans. Your students should have a pretty good grasp of what to look for by now and can continue making entries on their own.)*

Lesson 43: Jonathan Helps David

Materials Needed
- Bible
- *Wisdom for Life* (grades 7–12)

Family: Ask students what they recall from last time's reading about Saul's rejection as king and David's anointing as the new king. Explain that even though David had been anointed, he still respected Saul's position and honored him as king, but Saul was suspicious. Read together 1 Samuel 17—19 and ask for an oral narration.

If desired, explain that some of the psalms David wrote tell in which situation he wrote them. Read together Psalm 59, starting with the note before verse 1 that explains how this psalm was written during the event that was just read in 1 Samuel.

Grades 7–12: Continue working on *Wisdom for Life* Proverbs study.

Tip: If your student has been reading Proverbs seven days a week, he should be ready to finish up the second topic and begin a new one this week. Assign a written narration that summarizes his findings if desired.

Book of Centuries Timeline

David anointed king of Israel (1063 B.C.)

Book of Centuries Timeline

Lesson 44: The Music of Tyrtaeus

Materials Needed
- *The Story of the Greeks*
- *Herodotus and the Road to History* (grades 4–6)
- *Black Ships Before Troy* (grades 7–9)
- *The Odyssey* (grades 10–12)

Family: Ask students what they recall from last time's reading about the war between the Spartans and the Messenians. Read together *The Story of the Greeks*, chapters 30 and 31, "The Music of Tyrtaeus" and "Aristomenes' Escape." Ask for an oral narration.

Grades 4–6: Read together or assign as independent reading *Herodotus and the Road to History*, chapter 9, "To Thurii." Ask for an oral or written narration.

Grades 7–9: Read together or assign as independent reading *Black Ships Before Troy*, chapter 15, "Warrior Women," and ask for an oral or written narration.

Grades 10–12: Read together or assign as independent reading *The Odyssey*, book 17, and ask for an oral or written narration.

Lesson 45: The Olympic Games

Materials Needed
- *The Story of the Greeks*
- *Our Little Spartan Cousin of Long Ago* (grades 1–3 or 1–6)
- *Black Ships Before Troy* (grades 7–9)
- *The Odyssey* (grades 10–12)

Olympic Games begin record-keeping (776 B.C.)

Family: Ask students if they have heard of the Olympics and what they know about those games. Explain that today's reading will tell about how those games began in Ancient Greece thousands of years ago. Read together *The Story of the Greeks*, chapters 32 and 33, "The Olympic Games" and "Milo of Croton." Ask for an oral narration.

Grades 1–3 or 1–6: Read together *Our Little Spartan Cousin of Long Ago*, chapter 9, "New Adventures."

Grades 7–9: Read together or assign as independent reading *Black Ships Before Troy*, chapter 16, "The Death of Achilles," and ask for an oral or written narration.

Grades 10–12: Read together or assign as independent reading *The Odyssey*, book 18, and ask for an oral or written narration.

Book of Centuries Timeline

> *Tip: Make sure older children are up to date with their* Discovering Doctrine *notebooks and their Book of Centuries entries.*

Lesson 46: David Flees from Saul

Materials Needed

- Bible
- *Wisdom for Life* (grades 7–12)

Family: Ask students what they recall from last time's reading about Saul's jealousy of David. Explain that today's reading will show how Jonathan, Saul's son who would have been next in line to the throne, tried to help David. Read together 1 Samuel 20 and 21 and ask for an oral narration.

If desired, read together Psalms 56 and 34, including the note at the beginning of each.

Grades 7–12: Continue working on *Wisdom for Life* Proverbs study.

Lesson 47: Saul Kills the Priests & Visit 10 to the Middle East

Materials Needed

- Bible
- *Visits to the Middle East*
- *Wisdom for Life* (grades 7–12)

Family: Ask students what they recall from last time's reading about David and Jonathan. Explain that today's reading will show just how much Saul's jealousy was driving him. Read together 1 Samuel 22 and ask for an oral narration.

If desired, read together Psalms 142 and 52, including the note at the beginning of each. Also read together 2 Samuel 23:8–39 that gives more details about David's mighty men and their exploits.

> *Tip: Notice that the final man listed as a loyal member of David's band is Uriah the Hittite. See if the students make a mental connection when you get to lesson 72 and read how David tried to kill Uriah to cover David's sin.*

Family: Complete Visit 10 in *Visits to the Middle East.*

Grades 7–12: Continue working on *Wisdom for Life* Proverbs study.

Book of Centuries Timeline

Lesson 48: Saul Pursues David

Materials Needed
- Bible
- *Wisdom for Life* (grades 7–12)

Family: Ask students what they recall from last time's reading about Saul's pursuing David. Explain that David was on the run for many years, but God always protected him. Read together 1 Samuel 23 and ask for an oral narration.

If desired, read together Psalms 63 and 54, including the note at the beginning of each.

Grades 7–12: Continue working on *Wisdom for Life* Proverbs study.

Lesson 49: The Jealous Athlete

Materials Needed
- *The Story of the Greeks*
- *Herodotus and the Road to History,* if needed (grades 4–6)
- *Black Ships Before Troy* (grades 7–9)
- *The Odyssey* (grades 10–12)

Family: Ask students what they recall from last time's reading about the Olympic Games and the legendary athlete, Milo of Croton. Read together *The Story of the Greeks*, chapters 34 and 35, "The Jealous Athlete" and "The Girls' Games." Ask for an oral narration.

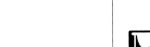

Herodotus writes his histories (c. 447 B.C.)

Grades 4–6: Use today to catch up on any assigned reading in *Herodotus and the Road to History* if needed.

Grades 7–9: Read together or assign as independent reading *Black Ships Before Troy,* chapter 17, "Poisoned Arrow," and ask for an oral or written narration.

Grades 10–12: Read together or assign as independent reading *The Odyssey,* book 19, and ask for an oral or written narration.

Lesson 50: The Bloody Laws of Draco

Materials Needed
- *The Story of the Greeks*
- *Our Little Spartan Cousin of Long Ago* (grades 1–3 or 1–6)

- *Black Ships Before Troy* (grades 7–9)
- *The Odyssey* (grades 10–12)

Family: Ask students what they recall about the king Codrus and how he sacrificed himself to spur Athens to victory. Read together *The Story of the Greeks*, chapter 36, "The Bloody Laws of Draco." Ask for an oral narration.

Grades 1–3 or 1–6: Read together *Our Little Spartan Cousin of Long Ago*, chapter 10, "A Vacancy Filled."

Grades 7–9: Read together or assign as independent reading *Black Ships Before Troy*, chapter 18, "The Wooden Horse," and ask for an oral or written narration.

Grades 10–12: Read together or assign as independent reading *The Odyssey*, book 20, and ask for an oral or written narration.

Reminder: *If you want to do an optional hands-on project for lesson 59 or 60, start collecting the materials you will need.*

Reminder: *Start collecting the resources you will need for Term 2. See page 49 for details.*

Book of Centuries Timeline

Draco's bloody laws enacted in Athens (602 B.C.)

Lesson 51: David Spares Saul's Life

Materials Needed
- Bible
- *Wisdom for Life* (grades 7–12)

Family: Ask the students how they would feel if they had been rightfully anointed king, yet the present king kept trying to kill them. Explain that in today's reading David had an opportunity to turn the tables. Read together 1 Samuel 24 and ask for an oral narration.

If desired, read together Psalm 57, including the note at the beginning.

Grades 7–12: Continue working on *Wisdom for Life* Proverbs study.

Lesson 52: Abigail and Nabal & Visit 11 to the Middle East

Materials Needed
- Bible
- *Visits to the Middle East*
- *Wisdom for Life* (grades 7–12)

Book of Centuries Timeline

Family: Ask students what they recall from last time's reading about how David spared Saul's life. Explain that when a company of men are on the run, they can sometimes act rudely and take whatever they find along the way, but David's company was not like that; they were careful of others' property. Read together 1 Samuel 25 and ask for an oral narration.

Family: Complete Visit 11 in *Visits to the Middle East.*

Grades 7–12: Continue working on *Wisdom for Life* Proverbs study.

Lesson 53: David Again Spares Saul's Life

Materials Needed

- Bible
- *Wisdom for Life* (grades 7–12)

Family: Ask students what they recall from last time's reading about the foolish Nabal and his wife Abigail. Explain that sometimes the people who lived in the area would tell Saul where they had seen David. Read together 1 Samuel 26 and 27 and ask for an oral narration.

Grades 7–12: Continue working on *Wisdom for Life* Proverbs study.

Lesson 54: The Laws of Solon

Materials Needed

- *The Story of the Greeks*
- *Black Ships Before Troy* (grades 7–9)
- *The Odyssey* (grades 10–12)

Laws of Solon reform Athens (593 B.C.)

Family: Ask students what they recall from last time's reading about the bloody laws of Draco and the action that the archon Megacles took on the rebels. Read together *The Story of the Greeks*, chapter 37, "The Laws of Solon." Ask for an oral narration.

Grades 7–9: Read together or assign as independent reading *Black Ships Before Troy,* chapter 19, "The Fall of Troy," and ask for an oral or written narration.

Grades 10–12: Read together or assign as independent reading *The Odyssey,* book 21, and ask for an oral or written narration.

Lesson 55: The First Plays

Materials Needed

- *The Story of the Greeks*
- *The Stuff They Left Behind: From the Days of Ancient Greece*
- *Our Little Spartan Cousin of Long Ago* (grades 1–3 or 1–6)
- *Black Ships Before Troy*, if needed (grades 7–9)
- *The Odyssey* (grades 10–12)

Family: Ask students what they recall from last time's reading about the laws of Solon. Read together *The Story of the Greeks*, chapter 38, "The First Plays." As you read about the amphitheater, display and discuss the picture in the book and the photograph from *The Stuff They Left Behind: From the Days of Ancient Greece.* At the end of the chapter, ask for an oral narration.

Grades 1–3 or 1–6: Read together *Our Little Spartan Cousin of Long Ago,* chapter 11, "A Pledge and a Chase."

Grades 7–9: Use today to catch up on any assigned reading in *Black Ships Before Troy* if needed.

Grades 10–12: Read together or assign as independent reading *The Odyssey,* book 22, and ask for an oral or written narration.

Tip: Make sure older children are up to date with their Discovering Doctrine *notebooks and their Book of Centuries entries.*

Lesson 56: Joshua Catch Up or Exam

Materials Needed

- Bible (if doing catch-up reading)

Family: Use this day to catch up on any reading you need to finish, or use the questions below for the students' exam on Joshua.

Tip: Exams in a Charlotte Mason school require no "cramming" or preparation. You may be pleasantly surprised at what your students remember with no prompting.

Grades 1–3: Tell the story of Joshua and the walls of Jericho.
Grades 4–6: Tell all you know about the cities of refuge. What was their purpose and how were they situated in the land? (Note: You don't need to require the child to recall the name of each town that was designated a city of refuge. The simple fact that they were scattered throughout the land will suffice.)
Grades 7–9: Describe what you consider to be Joshua's hardest battle in

Book of Centuries Timeline

Book of Centuries Timeline

conquering Canaan and tell why you think it was his hardest.
Grades 10–12: "Choose you this day whom ye will serve." Who gave that challenge, to whom, and why?

Tip: *You may want to assign the older students to write their exam answers. Younger students may do oral exams; you might want to write or type their answers as they tell what they know. Or, if you have students in more than one grade level, you might allow them to do their exams orally in a group. That way the older can hear the younger, and the younger can hear the older.*

Grades 7–12: If older students have not yet written their narrations for the Proverbs studies they have done, you may want to use this week for them to catch up on that assignment.

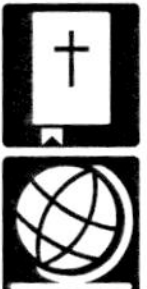

Lesson 57: Judges Catch Up or Exam & Visit 12 to the Middle East

Materials Needed

- Bible (if doing catch-up reading)
- *Visits to the Middle East*

Family: Use this day to catch up on any reading you need to finish, or use the questions below for the students' exam on Judges.
Grades 1–3: Find two objects around the house that remind you of two judges you studied. Tell about each judge.
Grades 4–6: Tell the story of Ruth.
Grades 7–9: Describe fully the repetitive cycle seen throughout the book of Judges.
Grades 10–12: "Out of the eater came forth meat, and out of the strong came forth sweetness." Who gave this riddle and on what occasion? Tell all you know about the speaker and the circumstances.

Family: Complete Visit 12 in *Visits to the Middle East.*

Lesson 58: 1 Samuel Catch Up or Exam

Materials Needed

- Bible (if doing catch-up reading)

Family: Use this day to catch up on any reading you need to finish, or use the questions below for the students' exam on 1 Samuel (studied so far).
Grades 1–3: Tell the story of how David was anointed king.

Grades 4–6: Tell all you know about Israel's first king, Saul.
Grades 7–9: "And Jonathan loved him as his own soul." Of whom was this said? Tell a story of Jonathan's love.
Grades 10–12: Compare Samuel and Saul, considering their characters and actions.

Tip: *If your student has been reading Proverbs five days a week, he should be ready to finish up the second topic in Wisdom for Life and begin a new one this week. Assign a written narration that summarizes his findings if desired.*

Book of Centuries Timeline

Lesson 59: Ancient Greece Catch Up, Project, or Exam

Materials Needed

- *The Story of the Greeks* (if doing catch-up reading)
- *The Odyssey* (grades 10–12)
- (optional) Materials for hands-on project

Family: Use this day to catch up on any reading you need to finish in *The Story of the Greeks*, or use the questions below for part of the students' exam on their Ancient Greece readings. You might also begin an optional hands-on project if you would prefer to do that instead.
Grades 1–3: Tell a story about a Greek hero.
Grades 4–6: Tell the story of Theseus and the Labyrinth.
Grades 7–9: When people today refer to someone's "Achilles' heel," what do they mean? Give the story behind that reference and explain it.
Grades 10–12: Tell all you know about the Trojan War.

Grades 10–12: Read together or assign as independent reading *The Odyssey*, book 23, and ask for an oral or written narration.

Optional Hands-On Project: Select a hands-on project from the Links and Tips page: http://simplycm.com/joshua-links

Lesson 60: Ancient Greece Catch Up, Project, or Exam

Materials Needed

- *The Story of the Greeks* (if doing catch-up reading)
- *The Odyssey* (grades 10–12)
- (optional) Materials for hands-on project

Book of Centuries Timeline

Family: Use this day to catch up on any reading you need to finish in *The Story of the Greeks*, or use the questions below for the students' exam on their Ancient Greece readings. You might also complete an optional hands-on project if you would prefer to do that instead.
Grades 1–3: Tell about life in Sparta.
Grades 4–6: Tell all you can recall about Herodotus.
Grades 7–9: Describe how the Olympic Games were started and give any anecdotes you recall connected with those ancient games.
Grades 10–12: Compare and contrast the laws of Draco and the laws of Solon.

Grades 10–12: Read together or assign as independent reading *The Odyssey,* book 24, and ask for an oral or written narration.

Optional Hands-On Project: Select a hands-on project from the Links and Tips page: http://simplycm.com/joshua-links)

Term 2

(12 weeks; 5 lessons/week)

Term 2 Book List

Family

- Bible
- *Material World* by Peter Menzel
- *The Story of the Greeks* by H. A. Guerber, edited by Christine Miller
- *The Stuff They Left Behind: From the Days of Ancient Greece* portfolio
- *Then and Now Bible Maps* from Rose Publishing
- *Visits to the Middle East* notebook by Sonya Shafer (one for each student)

Plus . . .

Grades 1–3

- *Our Little Athenian Cousin of Long Ago* by Julia Darrow Cowles
- *Our Little Spartan Cousin of Long Ago* by Julia Darrow Cowles

Grades 4–6

- *Archimedes and the Door of Science* by Jeanne Bendick
- *Our Little Athenian Cousin of Long Ago* by Julia Darrow Cowles (if desired)
- *Our Little Spartan Cousin of Long Ago* by Julia Darrow Cowles (if desired)

Grades 7–9

- Book of Centuries (one for each student)
- *Discovering Doctrine* by Sonya Shafer (one for each student)
- *The Wanderings of Odysseus* by Rosemary Sutcliff
- *Wisdom for Life: A Proverbs Bible Study* by Sonya Shafer (one for each student)
- *A Young Macedonian in the Army of Alexander the Great* by Alfred Church

Grades 10–12

- Book of Centuries (one for each student)
- *Discovering Doctrine* by Sonya Shafer (one for each student)
- *A Victor of Salamis* by William Stearns Davis
- *Wisdom for Life: A Proverbs Bible Study* by Sonya Shafer (one for each student)

Optional

- *The Big Picture Bible Time Line* by Carol Eide (grades 1–6)
- *A Child's Story Bible* by Catherine Vos (grades 1–3)
- Sheet of poster board and felt-tip markers (for Kings chart)
- Various materials for hands-on projects

What You Will Cover As a Family

Bible: *1 Samuel—2 Kings (Note: The books of 1 and 2 Chronicles recount mainly the same events presented in 2 Samuel and 1 and 2 Kings.)*

Geography: *Middle East, with special emphasis on Uzbekistan and Iraq*

History: *Ancient Greece, from Pisistratus through Epaminondas*

Term 2 At a Glance

	Family	Grades 1–3	Grades 4–6	Grades 7–9	Grades 10–12
			Week 1, Lessons 61–65		
Bible	1, 2 Samuel			Proverbs Study	Proverbs Study
History	Story of the Greeks, ch. 39–42	Our Little Spartan Cousin, ch. 12		The Wanderings of Odysseus, ch. 1, 2	A Victor of Salamis, ch. 1, 2
Geography	Visits to the Middle East, Visit 13				
			Week 2, Lessons 66–70		
Bible	2 Samuel			Proverbs Study	Proverbs Study
History	Story of the Greeks, ch. 43–46	Our Little Spartan Cousin, ch. 13		The Wanderings of Odysseus, ch. 3, 4	A Victor of Salamis, ch. 3–6
Geography	Visits to the Middle East, Visit 14				
			Week 3, Lessons 71–75		
Bible	2 Samuel			Proverbs Study	Proverbs Study
History	Story of the Greeks, ch. 47–49	Our Little Spartan Cousin, ch. 14	Archimedes, ch. 1	The Wanderings of Odysseus, ch. 5, 6	A Victor of Salamis, ch. 7–10
Geography	Visits to the Middle East, Visit 15				
			Week 4, Lessons 76–80		
Bible	2 Samuel			Proverbs Study	Proverbs Study
History	Story of the Greeks, ch. 50–53	Our Little Spartan Cousin, ch. 15	Archimedes, ch. 2A	The Wanderings of Odysseus, ch. 7, 8	A Victor of Salamis, ch. 11–14
Geography	Visits to the Middle East, Visit 16				
			Week 5, Lessons 81–85		
Bible	2 Samuel			Proverbs Study	Proverbs Study
History	Story of the Greeks, ch. 54–57	Our Little Spartan Cousin, ch. 16	Archimedes, ch. 2B	The Wanderings of Odysseus, ch. 9, 10	A Victor of Salamis, ch. 15–18
Geography	Visits to the Middle East, Visit 17				
			Week 6, Lessons 86–90		
Bible	1 Kings			Proverbs Study	Proverbs Study
History	Story of the Greeks, ch. 58–61	Our Little Spartan Cousin, ch. 17	Archimedes, ch. 3A	The Wanderings of Odysseus, ch. 11, 12	A Victor of Salamis, ch. 19–22
Geography	Visits to the Middle East, Visit 18				

Use this chart to see what your family and each of your students will be studying week by week during this term. You will also be able to see when each book is scheduled to be used.

	Family	Grades 1–3	Grades 4–6	Grades 7–9	Grades 10–12
Week 7, Lessons 91–95					
Bible	1 Kings; Ecclesiastes			Proverbs Study	Proverbs Study
History	Story of the Greeks, ch. 62–65	Our Little Spartan Cousin, ch. 18	Archimedes, ch. 3B	The Wanderings of Odysseus, ch. 13, 14	A Victor of Salamis, ch. 23–26
Geography	Visits to the Middle East, Visit 19				
Week 8, Lessons 96–100					
Bible	1 Kings			Proverbs Study	Proverbs Study
History	Story of the Greeks, ch. 66–69	Our Little Athenian Cousin, ch. 1	Archimedes, ch. 4A	The Wanderings of Odysseus, ch. 15	A Victor of Salamis, ch. 27–30
Geography	Visits to the Middle East, Visit 20				
Week 9, Lessons 101–105					
Bible	1, 2 Kings			Proverbs Study	Proverbs Study
History	Story of the Greeks, ch. 70–73	Our Little Athenian Cousin, ch. 2	Archimedes, ch. 4B	A Young Macedonian, ch. 1, 2	A Victor of Salamis, ch. 31–34
Geography	Visits to the Middle East, Visit 21				
Week 10, Lessons 106–110					
Bible	2 Kings; Obadiah			Proverbs Study	Proverbs Study
History	Story of the Greeks, ch. 74–77	Our Little Athenian Cousin, ch. 3	Archimedes, ch. 5A	A Young Macedonian, ch. 3, 4	A Victor of Salamis, ch. 35–38
Geography	Visits to the Middle East, Visit 22				
Week 11, Lessons 111–115					
Bible	2 Kings			Proverbs Study	Proverbs Study
History	Story of the Greeks, ch. 78–81	Our Little Athenian Cousin, ch. 4	Archimedes, ch. 5B	A Young Macedonian, ch. 5, 6	A Victor of Salamis, ch. 39–41
Geography	Visits to the Middle East, Visit 23				
Week 12, Lessons 116–120					
Bible	Exam or Catch Up			Proverbs Study	Proverbs Study
History	Exam or Catch Up or Project				
Geography	Visits to the Middle East, Visit 24				

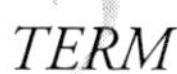

Lesson 61: Saul and the Witch of Endor

Book of Centuries Timeline

Materials Needed

- Bible
- *Wisdom for Life* (grades 7–12)

Family: Ask students how they would rate Saul's kingship so far. Encourage them to give the reasons for their ratings, thus reviewing previous chapters in 1 Samuel. Explain that in today's reading Saul once again transgressed God's Law. Read Deuteronomy 18:9–14, which gives God's prohibition of witches and seeking to communicate with those who have died. Then read together 1 Samuel 28 and ask for an oral narration.

Grades 7–12: Continue working on *Wisdom for Life* Proverbs study.

Lesson 62: The Death of Saul & Visit 13 to the Middle East

Materials Needed

- Bible
- *Then and Now Bible Maps*
- *Visits to the Middle East*
- *Wisdom for Life* (grades 7–12)

Death of Saul (1055 B.C.)

Family: Ask students what they recall about Samuel's words to Saul in last time's reading. Explain that they will read the fulfilment of that dire warning today. Read together 1 Samuel 29—31. As the locations of Jezreel, the land of the Philistines (Philistia), the Negev, and the Amalekites (from Amalek) are mentioned, find them on map 9, Holy Land - Old Testament, in *Then and Now Bible Maps.* Ask for an oral narration.

Family: Complete Visit 13 in *Visits to the Middle East.*

Grades 7–12: Continue working on *Wisdom for Life* Proverbs study.

Lesson 63: David Laments Saul's Death

Materials Needed

- Bible
- *Wisdom for Life* (grades 7–12)

Family: Ask students what they recall from last time's reading about Saul's final battle against the Philistines. Ask students to guess how long David had been running from Saul. (8–10 years.) Explain that in today's reading they will find out how David reacted to the news of Saul's death. Read together 2 Samuel 1 and ask for an oral narration.

Book of Centuries Timeline

Grades 7–12: Continue working on *Wisdom for Life* Proverbs study.

 Lesson 64: The Tyrant Pisistratus

Materials Needed

- *The Story of the Greeks*
- *The Wanderings of Odysseus* (grades 7–9)
- *A Victor of Salamis* (grades 10–12)

Pisistratus the Tyrant rules in Athens (560 B.C.)

Family: Ask students what they recall about the laws of Solon in Athens. Write the word "tyrant" on a small white board or sheet of paper and show it to the students. Discuss what a tyrant is and explain that in today's reading the Athenians met with one by trickery. Read together *The Story of the Greeks*, chapters 39 and 40, "The Tyrant Pisistratus" and "The Tyrant's Insult." Ask for an oral narration.

Grades 7–9: Read together or assign as independent reading *The Wanderings of Odysseus,* Prologue and chapter 1, "The Sacker of Cities," and ask for an oral or written narration.

Grades 10–12: Read together or assign as independent reading *A Victor of Salamis,* chapter 1, "Glaucon the Beautiful."

 Lesson 65: Death of the Conspirators

Materials Needed

- *The Story of the Greeks*
- *Our Little Spartan Cousin of Long Ago* (grades 1–3 or 1–6)
- *The Wanderings of Odysseus* (grades 7–9)
- *A Victor of Salamis* (grades 10–12)

Family: Ask students what they recall about the tyrant Pisistratus and his sons and the insult they gave. Explain that today students will find out whether the two friends were successful in their plot. Read together *The Story of the Greeks*, chapters 41 and 42, "Death of the Conspirators" and "Hippias driven out of Athens." Ask for an oral narration.

Grades 1–3 or 1–6: Read together *Our Little Spartan Cousin of Long Ago*, chapter 12, "The Drill."

Grades 7–9: Read together or assign as independent reading *The Wanderings of Odysseus,* chapter 2, "The Cyclops," and ask for an oral or written narration.

Grades 10–12: Read together or assign as independent reading *A Victor of Salamis,* chapter 2, "The Athlete."

Book of Centuries Timeline

Lesson 66: David Becomes King over Judah

Materials Needed

- Bible
- *Wisdom for Life* (grades 7–12)

Family: Ask students what they recall from last time's reading about David's reaction to Saul and Jonathan's death. Discuss what a king might do if only certain people wanted him to be their king and others did not. Explain that they will discover how David handled that situation in today's reading. Read together 2 Samuel 2 and 3 and ask for an oral narration.

Grades 7–12: Continue working on *Wisdom for Life* Proverbs study.

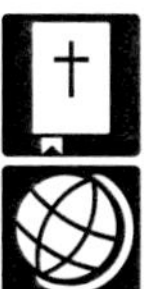

Lesson 67: David Becomes King over Israel & Visit 14 to the Middle East

Materials Needed

- Bible
- *Visits to the Middle East*
- *Wisdom for Life* (grades 7–12)

Family: Ask students what they recall from last time's reading about the struggle between those who wanted Saul's house to keep the kingship and those who wanted David to be king. Read together 2 Samuel 4 and 5 and ask for an oral narration.

David begins to reign (1055 B.C.)

Family: Complete Visit 14 in *Visits to the Middle East.*

Grades 7–12: Continue working on *Wisdom for Life* Proverbs study.

Tip: *If your student has been reading Proverbs seven days a week, he should be ready to finish up the third topic and begin a new one this week. Assign a written narration that summarizes his findings if desired.*

Lesson 68: The Ark Returns

Materials Needed

- Bible
- *Wisdom for Life* (grades 7–12)

Book of Centuries Timeline

Family: Ask students what they recall from last time's reading about how David became king over all Israel. Explain that David knew there was some unfinished business regarding the Ark of the Covenant. Review the events of 1 Samuel 4:1—7:2 as needed to refresh memories about where the Ark was and how it had gotten there. Read together 2 Samuel 6 and 7 and ask for an oral narration.

If desired, also read Psalm 18, including the note at the beginning of it that tells when David wrote it.

Grades 7–12: Continue working on *Wisdom for Life* Proverbs study.

 Lesson 69: The Great King

Materials Needed

- *The Story of the Greeks*
- *Then and Now Bible Maps*
- *The Wanderings of Odysseus* (grades 7–9)
- *A Victor of Salamis* (grades 10–12)

Family: Ask students what they recall about the plot to rid Athens of Hippias and Hipparchus and how it turned out. Look together at map 4 in *Then and Now Bible Maps*. Notice the distance between Greece (which is even farther west than Cyprus) and Persia. Notice also how the Persian Empire expanded over the years, as depicted on the three maps in yellow. Ask students what they suppose the king of Persia thought about events in Greece or if he even knew about it. Explain that they will find out in today's reading. Read together *The Story of the Greeks*, chapters 43 and 44, "The Great King" and "Hippias visits Darius." Ask for an oral narration.

Grades 7–9: Read together or assign as independent reading *The Wanderings of Odysseus,* chapter 3, "The Lord of the Winds," and ask for an oral or written narration.

Grades 10–12: Read together or assign as independent reading *A Victor of Salamis,* chapters 3 and 4, "The Hand of Persia" and "The Pentathlon."

 Lesson 70: Destruction of the Persian Host

Materials Needed

- *The Story of the Greeks*
- *Our Little Spartan Cousin of Long Ago* (grades 1–3 or 1–6)
- *The Wanderings of Odysseus* (grades 7–9)
- *A Victor of Salamis* (grades 10–12)

Family: Ask students what they recall from last time's reading about Hippias' and King Darius' reasons for attacking Greece. Read together *The Story of* *the Greeks,* chapters 45 and 46, "Destruction of the Persian Host" and "The Advance of the Second Host." When the text refers you to the map on page 17, be sure to follow along and locate Sardis, the Hellespont, Thrace, and other areas mentioned so students can better picture what happened. You can see the paths the various hosts took, both foot soldiers and fleets. Ask for an oral narration.

Grades 1–3 or 1–6: Read together *Our Little Spartan Cousin of Long Ago,* chapter 13, "The Days of Preparation."

Grades 7–9: Read together or assign as independent reading *The Wanderings of Odysseus,* chapter 4, "The Enchantress," and ask for an oral or written narration.

Grades 10–12: Read together or assign as independent reading *A Victor of Salamis,* chapters 5 and 6, "Hermione of Eleusis" and "Athens."

Tip: Make sure older children are up to date with their Discovering Doctrine *notebooks and their Book of Centuries entries.*

Book of Centuries Timeline

Persian War (494–479 B.C.)

Lesson 71: David and Mephibosheth

Materials Needed

- Bible
- *Wisdom for Life* (grades 7–12)

Family: Ask students what they recall from last time's reading about David's bringing the Ark back where it belonged and God's promise to him. Explain that many new kings would put to death all of the remaining relatives of the old king so they couldn't make a claim for the throne. In today's reading the students will see how David treated the remaining relatives of Saul and why. Read together 2 Samuel 9 and 10 and ask for an oral narration.

If desired, also read Psalm 60, including the note at the beginning.

Grades 7–12: Continue working on *Wisdom for Life* Proverbs study.

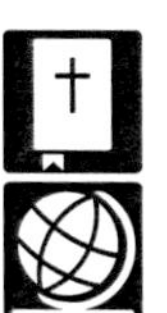

Lesson 72: David and Bathsheba & Visit 15 to the Middle East

Materials Needed

- Bible
- (optional) *A Child's Story Bible* (grades 1–3)
- *Visits to the Middle East*
- *Wisdom for Life* (grades 7–12)

Book of Centuries Timeline

Family: Ask students what they recall about David and his treatment of Mephibosheth. Explain that though David did many things right, he was still human, and today's reading will reveal a time when he grievously sinned. Read together 2 Samuel 11 and 12 for older children. For younger children, you may want to read the paraphrase of this passage in *A Child's Story Bible*, chapter 73. Ask for an oral narration.

If desired, also read Psalm 51, including the note at the beginning. Discuss why it is helpful to have the account of David's sin as well as his victories.

Family: Complete Visit 15 in *Visits to the Middle East.*

Grades 7–12: Continue working on *Wisdom for Life* Proverbs study.

 Lesson 73: Absalom Stirs Up Trouble

Materials Needed

- Bible
- *Wisdom for Life* (grades 7–12)

Absalom's rebellion (1023 B.C.)

Family: Ask students what they recall from last time's reading about David and Bathsheba. Explain that though David was victorious on the battlefield, his own family often caused him great heartache. Read together 2 Samuel 13, 14, and 15:1–12 for older children. If younger children are present, paraphrase 2 Samuel 13:1–22 by saying something like, "King David had many grown sons and daughters. One day his son Amnon grievously wronged Tamar, one of the daughters. Another son, Absalom, was angry with Amnon and vowed to get revenge in good time." Then pick up the Bible reading at 2 Samuel 13:23. Ask for an oral narration.

Grades 7–12: Continue working on *Wisdom for Life* Proverbs study.

 Lesson 74: The Battle of Marathon

Materials Needed

- *The Story of the Greeks*
- *The Stuff They Left Behind: From the Days of Ancient Greece*
- *Archimedes and the Door of Science* (grades 4–6)
- *The Wanderings of Odysseus* (grades 7–9)
- *A Victor of Salamis* (grades 10–12)

Family: Ask students what they recall from last time's reading about Athens' and Sparta's preparations to meet King Darius and his Persian host. Read together *The Story of the Greeks*, chapter 47, "The Battle of Marathon." Display and discuss the picture of the Helmet of Miltiades from *The Stuff They Left Behind: From the Days of Ancient Greece* portfolio.

Then read together *The Story of the Greeks*, chapter 48, "Miltiades' Disgrace." Ask for an oral narration of both chapters.

Grades 4–6: Read together or assign as independent reading *Archimedes and the Door of Science*, chapter 1, "Who Was Archimedes?" Ask for an oral or written narration.

Grades 7–9: Read together or assign as independent reading *The Wanderings of Odysseus,* chapter 5, "The Land of the Dead," and ask for an oral or written narration.

Grades 10–12: Read together or assign as independent reading *A Victor of Salamis,* chapters 7 and 8, "Democrates and the Tempter" and "On the Acropolis."

Book of Centuries Timeline

Battle of Marathon (490 B.C.)

Lesson 75: Aristides the Just

Materials Needed

- *The Story of the Greeks*
- *The Stuff They Left Behind: From the Days of Ancient Greece*
- *Our Little Spartan Cousin of Long Ago* (grades 1–3 or 1–6)
- *The Wanderings of Odysseus* (grades 7–9)
- *A Victor of Salamis* (grades 10–12)

Family: Ask students what they recall from last time's reading about Miltiades, his heroics at Marathon and his ultimate disgrace. Pose this question to the students: If King Darius were to plan another attack, which would be the best way to meet him: with a strong foot-soldier army or a strong navy of ships? Explain that this question caused great strife among the Athenians. Read together *The Story of the Greeks*, chapter 49, "Aristides the Just." Ask for an oral narration.

Display and discuss the picture of the Ostraca Pieces from *The Stuff They Left Behind: From the Days of Ancient Greece* portfolio.

Grades 1–3 or 1–6: Read together *Our Little Spartan Cousin of Long Ago*, chapter 14, "The Carnea."

Grades 7–9: Read together or assign as independent reading *The Wanderings of Odysseus,* chapter 6, "Sea Perils," and ask for an oral or written narration.

Grades 10–12: Read together or assign as independent reading *A Victor of Salamis,* chapters 9 and 10, "The Cyprian Triumphs" and "Democrates Resolves."

Book of Centuries Timeline

Lesson 76: David Flees from Absalom

Materials Needed

- Bible
- *Wisdom for Life* (grades 7–12)

Family: Ask students what they recall from last time's reading about Absalom and his treachery. Read together 2 Samuel 15:13–37 and chapters 16 and 17. Ask for an oral narration.

If desired, also read Psalm 3, including the note at the beginning.

Grades 7–12: Continue working on *Wisdom for Life* Proverbs study.

Lesson 77: Absalom Dies & Visit 16 to the Middle East

Materials Needed

- Bible
- *Visits to the Middle East*
- *Material World*
- *Wisdom for Life* (grades 7–12)

Family: Ask students what they recall from last time's reading about Absalom's move to steal the kingdom and David's reaction. Read together 2 Samuel 18:1—19:8 and ask for an oral narration.

Family: Complete Visit 16 in *Visits to the Middle East.*

Grades 7–12: Continue working on *Wisdom for Life* Proverbs study.

Lesson 78: David Returns to Jerusalem

Materials Needed

- Bible
- *Wisdom for Life* (grades 7–12)

Family: Ask students what they recall from last time's reading about Absalom's death and how David responded to the news. Explain that in today's reading David sought to return to Jerusalem. Read together 2 Samuel 19:9—20:26 and ask for an oral narration.

Grades 7–12: Continue working on *Wisdom for Life* Proverbs study.

Lesson 79: Two Noble Spartan Youths

Book of Centuries Timeline

Materials Needed

- *The Story of the Greeks*
- *Archimedes and the Door of Science* (grades 4–6)
- *The Wanderings of Odysseus* (grades 7–9)
- *A Victor of Salamis* (grades 10–12)

Family: Ask students what they recall from last time's reading about Aristides the Just, who was ostracized from Athens. Also discuss what the students recall about how Sparta and Athens treated the Persian messengers who had come demanding earth and water. Explain that Sparta soon repented of its actions in the face of another attack from Persia—an even larger one. Read together *The Story of the Greeks*, chapters 50 and 51, "Two Noble Spartan Youths" and "The Great Army." Ask for an oral narration.

Grades 4–6: Read together or assign as independent reading *Archimedes and the Door of Science*, the first half of chapter 2, "The World of Archimedes," pages 9–15. Ask for an oral or written narration.

Grades 7–9: Read together or assign as independent reading *The Wanderings of Odysseus,* chapter 7, "Telemachus Seeks His Father," and ask for an oral or written narration.

Grades 10–12: Read together or assign as independent reading *A Victor of Salamis,* chapters 11 and 12, "The Panathenaea" and "A Traitor to Hellas."

Lesson 80: Preparations for Defense

Materials Needed

- *The Story of the Greeks*
- *Our Little Spartan Cousin of Long Ago* (grades 1–3 or 1–6)
- *The Wanderings of Odysseus* (grades 7–9)
- *A Victor of Salamis* (grades 10–12)

Family: Ask students what they recall from last time's reading about Xerxes' great army and its approach to Greece. Ask students what they think Athens should have done in this situation. Read together *The Story of the Greeks*, chapters 52 and 53, "Preparations for Defense" and "Leonidas at Thermopylae." Ask for an oral narration.

Grades 1–3 or 1–6: Read together *Our Little Spartan Cousin of Long Ago*, chapter 15, "The Truce-Bearers."

Grades 7–9: Read together or assign as independent reading *The Wanderings of Odysseus,* chapter 8, "Farewell to Calypso," and ask for an oral or written narration.

Book of Centuries Timeline

Grades 10–12: Read together or assign as independent reading *A Victor of Salamis,* chapters 13 and 14, "The Disloyalty of Phormio" and "Mardonius the Persian."

> ***Tip:*** *Make sure older children are up to date with their* Discovering Doctrine *notebooks and their Book of Centuries entries.*

Lesson 81: David's Victory against Gibeon

Materials Needed

- Bible
- *Wisdom for Life* (grades 7–12)

Family: Ask each student to tell about an event from David's life. Explain that the final chapters of 2 Samuel recount some other events that happened sometime during David's reign. Read together 2 Samuel 21 and 22 and ask for an oral narration.

> ***Tip:*** *Second Samuel 22 is very similar to Psalm 18, which you may have read in an earlier lesson. You may want to point out this fact and not read the whole thing again.*

Grades 7–12: Continue working on *Wisdom for Life* Proverbs study.

Lesson 82: David's Last Days & Visit 17 to the Middle East

Materials Needed

- Bible
- *Visits to the Middle East*
- *Wisdom for Life* (grades 7–12)

Family: Explain that God rarely told Israel's leaders to count their fighting men. Discuss why that action might prove to be a snare to the leader. Explain that in today's reading King David took a count, with disastrous results, and then appointed the next king. Read together 2 Samuel 24 and 1 Kings 1 and ask for an oral narration.

Family: Complete Visit 17 in *Visits to the Middle East.*

Grades 7–12: Continue working on *Wisdom for Life* Proverbs study.

Lesson 83: Preparations for the Temple

Materials Needed
- Bible
- *Then and Now Bible Maps*
- *Wisdom for Life* (grades 7–12)

Family: Explain that though it would be Solomon's job to build a temple for the Lord, one of David's final tasks was to help with the preparations. Read together 1 Chronicles 22, 28, and 29 and ask for an oral narration.

Look together at map 9, Holy Land - Old Testament, of Then and Now Bible Maps. The map 8 overlay compares the size of Saul's kingdom, David's kingdom, and Solomon's kingdom. Ask the students what they notice about the three kingdoms' territories.

Tip: Be careful not to play "guess what the teacher is thinking" with this exercise. Simply open it up for the students to observe and to comment.

Grades 7–12: Continue working on *Wisdom for Life* Proverbs study.

Lesson 84: Death of Leonidas

Materials Needed
- *The Story of the Greeks*
- *Archimedes and the Door of Science* (grades 4–6)
- *The Wanderings of Odysseus* (grades 7–9)
- *A Victor of Salamis* (grades 10–12)

Family: Ask students what they recall from last time's reading about Thermopylae and the soldiers who there met Xerxes' host. Explain that today the students will find out how that conflict ended. Read together *The Story of the Greeks*, chapters 54 and 55, "Death of Leonidas" and "The Burning of Athens." Ask for an oral narration.

Grades 4–6: Read together or assign as independent reading *Archimedes and the Door of Science*, the last half of chapter 2, "The World of Archimedes," pages 16–23. Ask for an oral or written narration.

Grades 7–9: Read together or assign as independent reading *The Wanderings of Odysseus,* chapter 9, "The King's Daughter," and ask for an oral or written narration.

Grades 10–12: Read together or assign as independent reading *A Victor of Salamis,* chapters 15 and 16, "The Lotus-Eating at Sardis" and "The Coming of Xerxes the God-King."

Book of Centuries Timeline

Solomon begins to reign (1015 B.C.)

Battle of Thermopylae; Leonidas (480 B.C.)

Book of Centuries Timeline

Lesson 85: The Battles of Salamis and Plataea

Materials Needed

- *The Story of the Greeks*
- *Our Little Spartan Cousin of Long Ago* (grades 1–3 or 1–6)
- *The Wanderings of Odysseus* (grades 7–9)
- *A Victor of Salamis* (grades 10–12)

Family: Ask students what they recall from last time's reading about the Persian hosts' advance and the Greeks' plans in response. Read together *The Story of the Greeks*, chapters 56 and 57, "The Battles of Salamis and Plataea" and "The Rebuilding of Athens." Ask for an oral narration.

Grades 1–3 or 1–6: Read together *Our Little Spartan Cousin of Long Ago*, chapter 16, "Earth and Water."

Grades 7–9: Read together or assign as independent reading *The Wanderings of Odysseus,* chapter 10, "The Phaeacian Games," and ask for an oral or written narration.

Grades 10–12: Read together or assign as independent reading *A Victor of Salamis,* chapters 17 and 18, "The Charming by Roxana" and "Democrates's Troubles Return."

Lesson 86: Solomon Asks for Wisdom

Materials Needed

- Bible
- *Wisdom for Life* (grades 7–12)

Family: Ask students what they recall from last time's reading about the transition in the kingdom of Israel. Discuss what students would most like to have if they were put in charge after King David like Solomon was. Read together 1 Kings 3 and 4:29–34 and ask for an oral narration.

Grades 7–12: Continue working on *Wisdom for Life* Proverbs study.

Lesson 87: Solomon Builds the Temple & Visit 18 to the Middle East

Materials Needed

- Bible
- *Visits to the Middle East*
- *Wisdom for Life* (grades 7–12)

Family: Ask students what they recall from last time's reading about King Solomon's wisdom. Explain that in today's reading Solomon fulfilled the project of building the Temple. Read together 1 Kings 5; 6:1, 37, 38; 7:1, 51; and chapter 8 and ask for an oral narration.

Family: Complete Visit 18 in *Visits to the Middle East.*

Grades 7–12: Continue working on *Wisdom for Life* Proverbs study.

Book of Centuries Timeline

Solomon dedicates the Temple (1004 B.C.)

Lesson 88: The Queen of Sheba Visits

Materials Needed

- Bible
- *Wisdom for Life* (grades 7–12)

Family: Ask students what they recall from last time's reading about the building of the Temple. Explain that Solomon's kingdom and wealth increased, and so did his fame. Read together 1 Kings 9 and 10 and ask for an oral narration.

If desired, also read Psalm 72, including the note at the beginning.

Grades 7–12: Continue working on *Wisdom for Life* Proverbs study.

Tip: *If your student has been reading Proverbs seven days a week, he should be ready to finish up the fourth topic and begin a new one this week. Assign a written narration that summarizes his findings if desired.*

Lesson 89: Death of Pausanias

Materials Needed

- *The Story of the Greeks*
- *Archimedes and the Door of Science* (grades 4–6)
- *The Wanderings of Odysseus* (grades 7–9)
- *A Victor of Salamis* (grades 10–12)

Family: Ask students what they recall from last time's reading about the victory over Persia and the rebuilding of Athens. Explain that this was not the last time Greece had dealings with Persia. In today's reading students will hear how Persia continued to touch the lives of various Greek men. Read together *The Story of the Greeks*, chapters 58 and 59, "Death of Pausanias" and "Cimon improves Athens." Ask for an oral narration.

Grades 4–6: Read together or assign as independent reading *Archimedes and the Door of Science*, the first half of chapter 3, "Alexandria!," pages 24–32. Ask for an oral or written narration.

Book of Centuries Timeline

Grades 7–9: Read together or assign as independent reading *The Wanderings of Odysseus,* chapter 11, "Return to Ithaca," and ask for an oral or written narration.

Grades 10–12: Read together or assign as independent reading *A Victor of Salamis,* chapters 19 and 20, "The Commandment of Xerxes" and "Thermopylae."

Lesson 90: The Earthquake

Materials Needed

- *The Story of the Greeks*
- *The Stuff They Left Behind: From the Days of Ancient Greece*
- *Our Little Spartan Cousin of Long Ago* (grades 1–3 or 1–6)
- *The Wanderings of Odysseus* (grades 7–9)
- *A Victor of Salamis* (grades 10–12)

The Golden Age of Athens under Pericles (469–428 B.C.)

Family: Ask students what they recall from last time's reading about Cimon and how he used his wealth for Athens. Read together *The Story of the Greeks,* chapters 60 and 61, "The Earthquake" and "The Age of Pericles." Ask for an oral narration.

Display and discuss the picture of the Parthenon from The Stuff They Left Behind: From the Days of Ancient Greece portfolio.

Grades 1–3 or 1–6: Read together *Our Little Spartan Cousin of Long Ago,* chapter 17, "A Runner from Marathon."

Grades 7–9: Read together or assign as independent reading *The Wanderings of Odysseus,* chapter 12, "The Beggar in the Corner," and ask for an oral or written narration.

Grades 10–12: Read together or assign as independent reading *A Victor of Salamis,* chapters 21 and 22, "The Three Hundred—And One" and "Mardonius Gives a Promise."

Reminder: *Get* Our Little Athenian Cousin of Long Ago *for lesson 100 for grades 1–3 or 1–6.*

Tip: *Make sure older children are up to date with their* Discovering Doctrine *notebooks and their Book of Centuries entries.*

Lesson 91: Solomon's Wives

Materials Needed

- Bible
- *Wisdom for Life* (grades 7–12)

Family: Ask students what they recall from previous readings about Solomon and his kingdom. Explain that Solomon was very wise and very wealthy, but he had one weakness that got him into trouble. Read together 1 Kings 11 and ask for an oral narration.

Grades 7–12: Continue working on *Wisdom for Life* Proverbs study.

Tip: If your student has been reading Proverbs five days a week, he should be ready to finish up the third topic and begin a new one this week. Assign a written narration that summarizes his findings if desired.

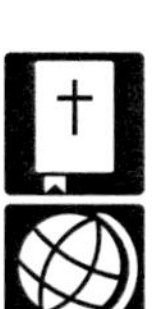

Lesson 92: Ecclesiastes & Visit 19 to the Middle East

Materials Needed

- Bible
- *Visits to the Middle East*
- *Wisdom for Life* (grades 7–12)

Family: Ask students what they recall from last time's reading about Solomon's weakness. Explain that Solomon wrote the book of Ecclesiastes at the end of his life, after his many wives had turned his heart away from the true God. The book describes how life is empty without God. Read Ecclesiastes 1:1–11 for a summary. Then read together these excerpts from Ecclesiastes and ask students to determine how Solomon tried to find meaning in life apart from God in each passage:

1:16–18 (wisdom, learning, education);
2:1–3 (fun, drinking responsibly);
2:4–11 (work, projects).

Explain that Solomon drew some conclusions from his experiences. Read together Ecclesiastes 3:1–8, 5:1–4, and 12:1–14, asking for an oral narration after each.

Family: Complete Visit 19 in *Visits to the Middle East.*

Grades 7–12: Continue working on *Wisdom for Life* Proverbs study.

Tip: Encourage older students to read through the rest of the book of Ecclesiastes to see what doctrinal truths they can find to record in Discovering Doctrine.

Lesson 93: The Kingdom Is Divided

Materials Needed

- Bible

Book of Centuries Timeline

Book of Centuries Timeline

The Kingdom is divided between Rehoboam and Jeroboam (975 B.C.)

- Sheet of poster board; felt-tip markers (two different colors)
- *Wisdom for Life* (grades 7–12)

Family: Ask students to recall what happened to the kingdom after Solomon's death. Read together 1 Kings 12 and 13. Start a Kings Chart with two lists: one column for the kings of Judah (the two southern tribes) and one column for the kings of Israel (the ten northern tribes). After each day's reading, have the students help you record under the appropriate column the name of any king you read about. Also, use two different colors for the kings: one color for those who were godly/good and another color for those were who ungodly/wicked. Ask the students to select which color to use for each king and explain why they chose that color, thus inviting a narration about the king's actions and character.

> ***Tip:*** *Some of the kings you read about will exhibit both godly and ungodly actions. You might use both colors to record their names—some letters in one color, other letters in the other color; or the top half of the letters in one color and the bottom half of the letters in the other color. Let the students determine how to portray each king, as that thought process will be a part of their narration.*

Grades 7–12: Continue working on *Wisdom for Life* Proverbs study.

 Lesson 94: The Teachings of Anaxagoras

Materials Needed

- *The Story of the Greeks*
- *Archimedes and the Door of Science* (grades 4–6)
- *The Wanderings of Odysseus* (grades 7–9)
- *A Victor of Salamis* (grades 10–12)

Peloponnesian War between Athens and Sparta (431–404 B.C.)

Family: Ask students what they recall from last time's reading about the Age of Pericles. Read together *The Story of the Greeks*, chapters 62 and 63, "The Teachings of Anaxagoras" and "Beginning of the Peloponnesian War." Ask for an oral narration.

Grades 4–6: Read together or assign as independent reading *Archimedes and the Door of Science*, the last half of chapter 3, "Alexandria!," pages 33–38. Ask for an oral or written narration.

Grades 7–9: Read together or assign as independent reading *The Wanderings of Odysseus,* chapter 13, "The Archery Contest," and ask for an oral or written narration.

Grades 10–12: Read together or assign as independent reading *A Victor* *of Salamis,* chapters 23 and 24, "The Darkest Hour" and "The Evacuation of Athens."

Book of Centuries Timeline

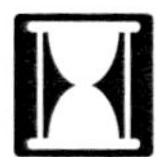

Lesson 95: Death of Pericles

Materials Needed

- *The Story of the Greeks*
- *Our Little Spartan Cousin of Long Ago* (grades 1–3 or 1–6)
- *The Wanderings of Odysseus* (grades 7–9)
- *A Victor of Salamis* (grades 10–12)

Family: Write the word "Peloponnesian" on a small white board or sheet of paper. Ask students what they recall from last time's reading about the Peloponnesian War and the part that superstition played in one of its battles. Read together *The Story of the Greeks,* chapters 64 and 65, "Death of Pericles" and "The Philosopher Socrates." Ask for an oral narration.

Grades 1–3 or 1–6: Read together *Our Little Spartan Cousin of Long Ago,* chapter 18, "For Sparta's Honor."

Grades 7–9: Read together or assign as independent reading *The Wanderings of Odysseus,* chapter 14, "The Slaying of the Suitors," and ask for an oral or written narration.

Grades 10–12: Read together or assign as independent reading *A Victor of Salamis,* chapters 25 and 26, "The Acropolis Flames" and "Themistocles is Thinking."

Reminder: *Make sure you have* A Young Macedonian in the Army of Alexander the Great *for lesson 104 for grades 7–9.*

Lesson 96: Idolatry and War

Materials Needed

- Bible
- Kings Chart; felt-tip markers
- *Wisdom for Life* (grades 7–12)

Family: Refer to your Kings Chart and see what the students remember about the most recent ones listed. Read together 1 Kings 14 and 15. Ask the students to help you record the kings from today's reading in the appropriate columns on the chart and with the correct colors. Have them explain their choices.

Book of Centuries Timeline

Grades 7–12: Continue working on *Wisdom for Life* Proverbs study.

Lesson 97: Ahab and Elijah & Visit 20 to the Middle East

Materials Needed

- Bible
- Kings Chart; felt-tip markers
- *Visits to the Middle East*
- *Wisdom for Life* (grades 7–12)

King Ahab reigns in Israel (918–897 B.C.)

Family: Ask students what they recall about the kings they have read about so far. Explain that in today's reading they will meet a prophet whom God sent to warn the king. Read together 1 Kings 16 and 17. Ask the students to help you record the kings from today's reading in the appropriate columns on the chart and with the correct colors. Have them explain their choices.

Family: Complete Visit 20 in *Visits to the Middle East.*

Grades 7–12: Continue working on *Wisdom for Life* Proverbs study.

Lesson 98: Elijah and the Prophets of Baal

Materials Needed

- Bible
- *The Stuff They Left Behind: From the Days of Ancient Greece*
- *Wisdom for Life* (grades 7–12)

Elijah defeats prophets of Baal on Mt. Carmel (906 B.C.)

Family: Ask students what they recall from last time's reading about Ahab and Elijah. Explain that in today's reading they will hear about a showdown between the true God and the false god Baal.

Display and discuss the picture of the Baal Bronze Figurine from *The Stuff They Left Behind: From the Days of Ancient Greece* portfolio. Then read together 1 Kings 18 and 19 and ask for an oral narration.

Grades 7–12: Continue working on *Wisdom for Life* Proverbs study.

Lesson 99: Socrates' Favorite Pupil

Materials Needed

- *The Story of the Greeks*
- *The Stuff They Left Behind: From the Days of Ancient Greece*

- *Archimedes and the Door of Science* (grades 4–6)
- *The Wanderings of Odysseus* (grades 7–9)
- *A Victor of Salamis* (grades 10–12)

Family: Ask students what they recall from last time's reading about Socrates, his thoughts, and his wife. Read together *The Story of the Greeks*, chapters 66 and 67, "Socrates' Favorite Pupil" and "Youth of Alcibiades." When you begin chapter 67 and read about Alcibiades' winning chariot races in the Olympic games, display and discuss the picture of the Charioteer of Delphi statue from *The Stuff They Left Behind: From the Days of Ancient Greece*. At the end of the chapter, ask for an oral narration.

Grades 4–6: Read together or assign as independent reading *Archimedes and the Door of Science*, the first half of chapter 4, "Archimedes and His Lever," pages 39–46. Ask for an oral or written narration.

Grades 7–9: Read together or assign as independent reading *The Wanderings of Odysseus,* chapter 15, "Peace in the Islands," and ask for an oral or written narration.

Grades 10–12: Read together or assign as independent reading *A Victor of Salamis,* chapters 27 and 28, "The Craft of Odysseus" and "Before the Death Grapple."

Lesson 100: Greek Colonies in Italy

Materials Needed

- *The Story of the Greeks*
- *Our Little Athenian Cousin of Long Ago* (grades 1–3 or 1–6)
- *The Wanderings of Odysseus*, if needed (grades 7–9)
- *A Victor of Salamis* (grades 10–12)

Family: Ask students what they recall from last time's reading about Alcibiades and his flambouyant ways. Explain that in today's reading students will discover the bad effect of his ambition. Read together *The Story of the Greeks*, chapters 68 and 69, "Greek Colonies in Italy" and "Alcibiades in Disgrace." Ask for an oral narration.

Grades 1–3 or 1–6: Read together *Our Little Athenian Cousin of Long Ago*, chapter 1, "The Guest-Friend."

Grades 7–9: Use today as needed to catch up on any assigned reading in *The Wanderings of Odysseus.*

Grades 10–12: Read together or assign as independent reading *A Victor of Salamis,* chapters 29 and 30, "Salamis" and "Themistocles Gives a Promise."

Book of Centuries Timeline

Book of Centuries Timeline

Tip: Make sure older children are up to date with their Discovering Doctrine *notebooks and their Book of Centuries entries.*

Lesson 101: Ahab Battles Ben-Hadad

Materials Needed

- Bible
- *Then and Now Bible Maps*
- *Wisdom for Life* (grades 7–12)

Family: Ask students what they recall from previous readings about King Ahab and Elijah. Locate Aram on map 9, Holy Land - Old Testament, in *Then and Now Bible Maps.* Explain that the king of Aram was about to pick a fight with Ahab. Read together 1 Kings 20 and ask for an oral narration.

Grades 7–12: Continue working on *Wisdom for Life* Proverbs study.

Lesson 102: Ahab Dies & Visit 21 to the Middle East

Materials Needed

- Bible
- Kings Chart; felt-tip markers
- *Visits to the Middle East*
- *Wisdom for Life* (grades 7–12)

Family: Ask students what they recall from last time's reading about King Ahab and his battles against the king of Aram. Explain that the accounts you will read today will give students even more insight into King Ahab's character. Read together 1 Kings 21 and 22. Ask the students to help you record the kings from today's reading in the appropriate columns on the chart and with the correct colors. Have them explain their choices.

Family: Complete Visit 21 in *Visits to the Middle East.*

Grades 7–12: Continue working on *Wisdom for Life* Proverbs study.

Lesson 103: Elijah Is Taken to Heaven

Elisha called as a prophet (896 B.C.)

Materials Needed

- Bible
- *Then and Now Bible Maps*
- *Wisdom for Life* (grades 7–12)

Book of Centuries Timeline

Family: Have students locate Moab on map 9 of *Then and Now Bible Maps.* Explain that as the kings of Israel and Judah grew weaker, the surrounding countries, that used to have to pay them tribute, began to rebel. Read together 2 Kings 1 and 2 and ask for an oral narration.

Grades 7–12: Continue working on *Wisdom for Life* Proverbs study.

Lesson 104: Death of Alcibiades

Materials Needed

- *The Story of the Greeks*
- *Archimedes and the Door of Science* (grades 4–6)
- *A Young Macedonian in the Army of Alexander the Great* (grades 7–9)
- *A Victor of Salamis* (grades 10–12)

Family: Ask students what they recall from last time's reading about the treachery and late repentance of Alcibiades. Explain that his story will continue in today's reading. Read together *The Story of the Greeks*, chapters 70 and 71, "Death of Alcibiades" and "The Overthrow of the Thirty Tyrants." Ask for an oral narration.

Grades 4–6: Read together or assign as independent reading *Archimedes and the Door of Science*, the last half of chapter 4, "Archimedes and His Lever," pages 47–53. Ask for an oral or written narration.

Grades 7–9: Read together or assign as independent reading *A Young Macedonian in the Army of Alexander the Great,* chapter 1, "A Wrong."

Grades 10–12: Read together or assign as independent reading *A Victor of Salamis,* chapters 31 and 32, "Democrates Surrenders" and "The Stranger in Troezene."

Lesson 105: Accusation of Socrates

Materials Needed

- *The Story of the Greeks*
- *Our Little Athenian Cousin of Long Ago* (grades 1–3 or 1–6)
- *A Young Macedonian in the Army of Alexander the Great* (grades 7–9)
- *A Victor of Salamis* (grades 10–12)

Execution of Socrates in Athens (399 B.C.)

Family: Ask students what they recall from last time's reading about the end of Alcibiades and the rule of the Thirty Tyrants that Sparta set up in Athens. Explain that Alcibiades' folly would continue to affect others even after his death. Read together *The Story of the Greeks*, chapters 72 and 73, "Accusation of Socrates" and "Death of Socrates." Ask for an oral narration.

Book of Centuries Timeline

Grades 1–3 or 1–6: Read together *Our Little Athenian Cousin of Long Ago*, chapter 2, "In the Market-Place."

Grades 7–9: Read together or assign as independent reading *A Young Macedonian in the Army of Alexander the Great,* chapter 2, "A Revenge."

Grades 10–12: Read together or assign as independent reading *A Victor of Salamis,* chapters 33 and 34, "What Befell on the Hillside" and "The Loyalty of Lampaxo."

Lesson 106: Elisha Begins His Ministry

Materials Needed

- Bible
- *The Stuff They Left Behind: From the Days of Ancient Greece*
- *Then and Now Bible Maps*
- *Wisdom for Life* (grades 7–12)

Family: Display and discuss the picture of the Mesha Stele from *The Stuff They Left Behind: From the Days of Ancient Greece* portfolio.

Ask students what they recall from previous readings about the prophet Elijah and his replacement, Elisha. Read together 2 Kings 3 and 4, locating Israel, Judah, Moab, and Edom on map 9 of Then and Now Bible Maps as you read about them. Ask for an oral narration.

Grades 7–12: Continue working on *Wisdom for Life* Proverbs study.

Lesson 107: Obadiah & Visit 22 to the Middle East

Materials Needed

- Bible
- *Then and Now Bible Maps*
- *Visits to the Middle East*
- *Material World*
- *Wisdom for Life* (grades 7–12)

Family: Explain that many prophets arose during the time of the kings with warnings and messages from the Lord. Some warnings were directed toward God's own people, to urge them to turn from some particular sin; others were directed toward Israel's enemies. Obadiah's prophecy warned Edom. Look together at *Then and Now Bible Maps*, map 9, to see where the people of Edom (descendants of Esau) lived. Read together the book of Obadiah and ask for an oral narration.

If you want to keep track of prophets on your Kings Chart, use a third color to add the name of each prophet where he belongs in the kings list.

Tip: Encourage older students to record any doctrinal truths from Obadiah in their Discovering Doctrine *books.*

Family: Complete Visit 22 in *Visits to the Middle East.*

Grades 7–12: Continue working on *Wisdom for Life* Proverbs study.

 Lesson 108: Naaman Is Healed

Materials Needed

- Bible
- *Then and Now Bible Maps*
- *Wisdom for Life* (grades 7–12)

Family: Ask students what they recall about the prophet Obadiah and his warning to Edom. Locate Aram on map 9 of *Then and Now Bible Maps* and explain that people in that country were hearing about Elisha, Elijah's replacement. Read together 2 Kings 5 and ask for an oral narration.

Grades 7–12: Continue working on *Wisdom for Life* Proverbs study.

 Lesson 109: The Defeat of Cyrus

Materials Needed

- *The Story of the Greeks*
- *Archimedes and the Door of Science* (grades 4–6)
- *A Young Macedonian in the Army of Alexander the Great* (grades 7–9)
- *A Victor of Salamis* (grades 10–12)

Family: Ask students what they recall from last time's reading about the accusation and death of Socrates. Explain that, though one of Socrates' pupils cast a shadow on him and on Athens, another of his pupils helped save 10,000 of his fellow Greeks from danger. Write "Xenophon" on a small white board or sheet of paper to display, then read together *The Story of the Greeks*, chapters 74 and 75, "The Defeat of Cyrus" and "The Retreat of the Ten Thousand." Ask for an oral narration.

Grades 4–6: Read together or assign as independent reading *Archimedes and the Door of Science*, the first half of chapter 5, "Archimedes and King Hiero's Crown," pages 54–61. Ask for an oral or written narration.

Book of Centuries Timeline

Retreat of the 10,000 (401 B.C.)

Book of Centuries Timeline

Grades 7–9: Read together or assign as independent reading *A Young Macedonian in the Army of Alexander the Great,* chapter 3, "Preparations."

Grades 10–12: Read together or assign as independent reading *A Victor of Salamis,* chapters 35 and 36, "Moloch Betrays the Phoenician" and "The Reading of the Riddle."

Lesson 110: Agesilaus in Asia

Materials Needed

- *The Story of the Greeks*
- *Our Little Athenian Cousin of Long Ago* (grades 1–3 or 1–6)
- *A Young Macedonian in the Army of Alexander the Great* (grades 7–9)
- *A Victor of Salamis* (grades 10–12)

Family: Ask students what they recall from last time's reading about Xenophon and the retreat of the 10,000. Explain that the retreat of the 10,000 spurred others to action. Write "Agesilaus" on a small white board or sheet of paper and display it. Explain that this Spartan was about to get involved. Read together *The Story of the Greeks*, chapters 76 and 77, "Agesilaus in Asia" and "A Strange Interview." Ask for an oral narration.

Grades 1–3 or 1–6: Read together *Our Little Athenian Cousin of Long Ago,* chapter 3, "The Acropolis."

Grades 7–9: Read together or assign as independent reading *A Young Macedonian in the Army of Alexander the Great,* chapter 4, "At Troy."

Grades 10–12: Read together or assign as independent reading *A Victor of Salamis,* chapters 37 and 38, "The Race to Save Hellas" and "The Council of Mardonius."

Reminder: *If you want to do an optional hands-on project for lesson 119 or 120, start collecting the materials you will need.*

Reminder: *Start collecting the resources you will need for Term 3.* *See page 83 for details.*

Tip: *Make sure older children are up to date with their* Discovering Doctrine *notebooks and their Book of Centuries entries.*

Lesson 111: More of Elisha's Ministry

Materials Needed

- Bible

Book of Centuries Timeline

- *Wisdom for Life* (grades 7–12)

Family: Ask students what they recall from previous readings about the marvelous works that the prophet Elisha performed. Explain that God continued to use Elisha as Ben-Hadad, king of Aram, attacked Israel again. Read together 2 Kings 6 and 7 and ask for an oral narration.

Grades 7–12: Continue working on *Wisdom for Life* Proverbs study.

Lesson 112: Jehu Anointed King of Israel & Visit 23 to the Middle East

Materials Needed

- Bible
- Kings Chart; felt-tip markers
- *Visits to the Middle East*
- *Wisdom for Life* (grades 7–12)

Family: Ask students what they recall from last time's reading about how God rescued Israel from Ben-Hadad's siege. Explain that that was not the last of Elisha's dealings with Aram. Read together 2 Kings 8 and 9. Ask the students to help you record the kings from today's reading in the appropriate columns on the chart and with the correct colors. Have them explain their choices.

Family: Complete Visit 23 in *Visits to the Middle East.*

Grades 7–12: Continue working on *Wisdom for Life* Proverbs study.

Lesson 113: Joash Is Saved

Materials Needed

- Bible
- Kings Chart; felt-tip markers
- *The Stuff They Left Behind: From the Days of Ancient Greece*
- *Wisdom for Life* (grades 7–12)

Family: Display and discuss the picture of the Obelisk of Shalmaneser II from *The Stuff They Left Behind: From the Days of Ancient Greece* portfolio.

Ask students what they recall about King Jehu. Read together 2 Kings 10 and 11. Ask the students to help you record the king from today's reading in the appropriate column on the chart and with the correct color. Have them explain their choices.

Grades 7–12: Continue working on *Wisdom for Life* Proverbs study.

Book of Centuries Timeline

Tip: *If your student has been reading Proverbs seven days a week, he should be ready to finish up the fifth topic and begin a new one this week. Assign a written narration that summarizes his findings if desired.*

 Lesson 114: The Peace of Antalcidas

Materials Needed

- *The Story of the Greeks*
- *Archimedes and the Door of Science* (grades 4–6)
- *A Young Macedonian in the Army of Alexander the Great* (grades 7–9)
- *A Victor of Salamis* (grades 10–12)

Family: Ask students what they recall from last time's reading about the Spartan general Agesilaus and how the Persian king planned to get the better of him. Read together *The Story of the Greeks*, chapters 78 and 79, "The Peace of Antalcidas" and "The Theban Friends." Ask for an oral narration.

Grades 4–6: Read together or assign as independent reading *Archimedes and the Door of Science*, the last half of chapter 5, "Archimedes and King Hiero's Crown," pages 62–69. Ask for an oral or written narration.

Grades 7–9: Read together or assign as independent reading *A Young Macedonian in the Army of Alexander the Great*, chapter 5, "At the Granicus."

Grades 10–12: Read together or assign as independent reading *A Victor of Salamis*, chapters 39 and 40, "The Avenging of Leonidas" and "The Song of the Furies."

 Lesson 115: Thebes Free Once More

Materials Needed

- *The Story of the Greeks*
- *Our Little Athenian Cousin of Long Ago* (grades 1–3 or 1–6)
- *A Young Macedonian in the Army of Alexander the Great* (grades 7–9)
- *A Victor of Salamis* (grades 10–12)

Family: Ask students what they recall from last time's reading about the shameful treaty that Antalcidas made with Persia and the actions Sparta took on Thebes. See if they remember anything about the two friends, one rich and one poor, who lived in Thebes: Pelopidas and Epaminondas. Explain that the two friends will play a significant role in today's reading. Read together *The Story of the Greeks*, chapters 80 and 81, "Thebes Free Once More" and "The Battle of Leuctra." Ask for an oral narration.

Grades 1–3 or 1–6: Read together *Our Little Athenian Cousin of Long Ago*, chapter 4, "Preparing for the Festival."

Grades 7–9: Read together or assign as independent reading *A Young Macedonian in the Army of Alexander the Great,* chapter 6, "Halicarnassus."

Book of Centuries Timeline

Grades 10–12: Read together or assign as independent reading *A Victor of Salamis,* chapter 41, "The Brightness of Helios."

Lesson 116: 2 Samuel Catch Up or Exam

Materials Needed

- Bible (if doing catch-up reading)

Family: Use this day to catch up on any reading you need to finish, or use the questions below for the students' exam on 2 Samuel.
Grades 1–3: Draw a picture of an event from King David's reign and tell about it.
Grades 4–6: Tell the story of when the Ark of the Covenant returned to Jerusalem under King David's reign.
Grades 7–9: Tell all you know about King David's son, Absalom.
Grades 10–12: Select one of these psalms: Psalm 3, 18, 51, 60, or 72. Look up your selected psalm in your Bible and explain fully the event mentioned in its introductory note.

Tip: *You may want to assign the older students to write their exam answers. Younger students may do oral exams; you might want to write or type their answers as they tell what they know. Or, if you have students in more than one grade level, you might allow them to do their exams orally in a group. That way the older can hear the younger, and the younger can hear the older.*

Grades 7–12: If older students have not yet written their narrations for the Proverbs studies they have done, you may want to use this week for them to catch up on that assignment.

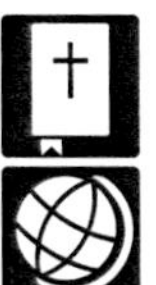

Lesson 117: 1 Kings Catch Up or Exam & Visit 24 to the Middle East

Materials Needed

- Bible (if doing catch-up reading)
- *Visits to the Middle East*

Family: Use this day to catch up on any reading you need to finish, or use the questions below for part of the students' exam on 1 Kings.

Book of Centuries Timeline

Grades 1–3: Tell the story of how God granted Solomon one request.
Grades 4–6: What have you noticed about the kings of the Divided Kingdom and their characters, as portrayed on your Kings Chart.
Grades 7–9: Describe King Solomon's achievements and failures.
Grades 10–12: Who said, "Remember now thy Creator in the days of thy youth"? Tell fully about the person and the context of this statement.

Family: Complete Visit 24 in *Visits to the Middle East.*

 Lesson 118: 1 Kings Catch Up or Exam

Materials Needed

- Bible (if doing catch-up reading)

Family: Use this day to catch up on any reading you need to finish, or use the questions below for the rest of the students' exam on 1 Kings.
Grades 1–3: Tell a story about the prophet Elijah or the prophet Elisha.
Grades 4–6: Write a poem about King Ahab and the prophet Elijah.
Grades 7–9: "Thou shalt see it with thine eyes, but shalt not eat thereof." Who made this statement? Tell fully the story behind it.
Grades 10–12: Describe the reign, characters, and deaths of King Ahab and Queen Jezebel and their effect on the kingdom of Israel. Tell about any of their descendants that you recall.

Tip: If your student has been reading Proverbs five days a week, he should be ready to finish up the fourth topic and begin a new one this week. Assign a written narration that summarizes his findings if desired.

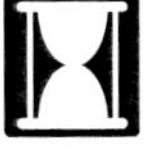 Lesson 119: Ancient Greece Catch-Up, Project, or Exam

Materials Needed

- (optional) Materials for hands-on project

Family: Use this day to catch up on any reading you need to finish, or use the questions below for part of the students' exam on their Ancient Greece readings. An optional hands-on project is also given if you would prefer to do that instead.
Grades 1–3: Tell a story of a battle in Ancient Greece.
Grades 4–6: A marathon is usually 26.2 miles in length. Tell the story behind that event and measurement.

Grades 7–9: When his friends expressed sorrow that he should die innocent, he replied, "What! would you have me die guilty?" Who made this reply and what do you know about him?
Grades 10–12: Explain the relationship between Sparta and Athens. What factors contributed to their conflicts and peaceful times? Cite examples from your reading.

Optional Hands-On Project: Select a hands-on project from the Links and Tips page: http://simplycm.com/joshua-links

Book of Centuries Timeline

Lesson 120: Ancient Greece Catch Up, Project, or Exam

Materials Needed

- (optional) Materials for hands-on project

Family: Use this day to catch up on any reading you need to finish, or use the questions below for the students' exam on their Ancient Greece readings. An optional hands-on project is also given if you would prefer to do that instead.
Grades 1–3: Tell about a person from Ancient Greece whom you admire.
Grades 4–6: Would you prefer life as a Spartan or an Athenian? Explain your answer.
Grades 7–9: Write a poem depicting one event from the wanderings of Odysseus.
Grades 10–12: Suppose Themistocles in the Battle of Salamis, write his diary for three days.

Optional Hands-On Project: Select a hands-on project from the Links and Tips page: http://simplycm.com/joshua-links

Term 3

(12 weeks; 5 lessons/week)

Term 3 Book List

Family

- Bible
- *Material World* **and** *Hungry Planet: What the World Eats* by Peter Menzel
- *The Story of the Greeks* by H. A. Guerber, edited by Christine Miller
- *The Stuff They Left Behind: From the Days of Ancient Greece* portfolio
- *Then and Now Bible Maps* from Rose Publishing
- *Visits to the Middle East* notebook (one for each student)

Plus . . .

Grades 1–3

- *Our Little Athenian Cousin of Long Ago* by Julia Darrow Cowles

Grades 4–6

- *Archimedes and the Door of Science* by Jeanne Bendick
- *Our Little Athenian Cousin of Long Ago* by Julia Darrow Cowles (if desired)

Grades 7–9

- Book of Centuries (one for each student)
- *Discovering Doctrine* by Sonya Shafer (one for each student)
- *Wisdom for Life: A Proverbs Bible Study* by Sonya Shafer (one for each student)
- *A Young Macedonian in the Army of Alexander the Great* by Alfred Church

Grades 10–12

- Book of Centuries (one for each student)
- *Discovering Doctrine* by Sonya Shafer (one for each student)
- *Plutarch's Lives*, biography of Alexander, by Plutarch
- *The Trial and Death of Socrates* by Plato
- *Wisdom for Life: A Proverbs Bible Study* by Sonya Shafer (one for each student)

Optional

- *The Big Picture Bible Time Line* by Carol Eide (grades 1–6)
- Sheet of poster board and felt-tip markers (for Kings chart)
- Various materials for hands-on projects

What You Will Cover As a Family

Bible: *2 Kings—Malachi*

Geography: *Middle East, with special emphasis on Kuwait*

History: *Ancient Greece, from Pelopidas through Greece becoming a Roman province*

Term 3 At a Glance

	Family	Grades 1–3	Grades 4–6	Grades 7–9	Grades 10–12
Week 1, Lessons 121–125					
Bible	2 Kings; Joel; Jonah			Proverbs Study	Proverbs Study
History	Story of the Greeks, ch. 82–85	Our Little Athenian Cousin, ch. 5	Archimedes and the Door of Science, ch. 6A	A Young Macedonian, ch. 7, 8	The Trial and Death of Socrates
Geography	Visits to the Middle East, Visit 25				
Week 2, Lessons 126–130					
Bible	2 Kings; Hosea; Amos; Micah			Proverbs Study	Proverbs Study
History	Story of the Greeks, ch. 86–89	Our Little Athenian Cousin, ch. 6	Archimedes, ch. 6B	A Young Macedonian, ch. 9, 10	The Trial and Death of Socrates
Geography	Visits to the Middle East, Visit 26				
Week 3, Lessons 131–135					
Bible	2 Kings; Isaiah			Proverbs Study	Proverbs Study
History	Story of the Greeks, ch. 90–93	Our Little Athenian Cousin, ch. 7	Archimedes, ch. 7	A Young Macedonian, ch. 11, 12	Plutarch's Alexander, 8 pages
Geography	Visits to the Middle East, Visit 27				
Week 4, Lessons 136–140					
Bible	2 Kings; Nahum; Zephaniah; Habakkuk			Proverbs Study	Proverbs Study
History	Story of the Greeks, ch. 94–97	Our Little Athenian Cousin, ch. 8	Archimedes, ch. 8	A Young Macedonian, ch. 13, 14	Plutarch's Alexander, 8 pages
Geography	Visits to the Middle East, Visit 28				
Week 5, Lessons 141–145					
Bible	2 Kings; Jeremiah; Ezekiel; Lamentations			Proverbs Study	Proverbs Study
History	Story of the Greeks, ch. 98–101	Our Little Athenian Cousin, ch. 9	Archimedes, ch. 9	A Young Macedonian, ch. 15, 16	Plutarch's Alexander, 8 pages
Geography	Visits to the Middle East, Visit 29				
Week 6, Lessons 146–150					
Bible	Daniel			Proverbs Study	Proverbs Study
History	Story of the Greeks, ch. 102–105	Our Little Athenian Cousin, ch. 10	Archimedes, ch. 10	A Young Macedonian, ch. 17, 18	Plutarch's Alexander, 8 pages
Geography	Visits to the Middle East, Visit 30				

Use this chart to see what your family and each of your students will be studying week by week during this term. You will also be able to see when each book is scheduled to be used.

	Family	Grades 1–3	Grades 4–6	Grades 7–9	Grades 10–12
Week 7, Lessons 151–155					
Bible	Daniel; Ezra			Proverbs Study	Proverbs Study
History	Story of the Greeks, ch. 106–109	Our Little Athenian Cousin, ch. 11	Archimedes, ch. 11	A Young Macedonian, ch. 19, 20	Plutarch's Alexander, 8 pages
Geography	Visits to the Middle East, Visit 31				
Week 8, Lessons 156–160					
Bible	Ezra; Esther			Proverbs Study	Proverbs Study
History	Story of the Greeks, ch. 110–111	Our Little Athenian Cousin, ch. 12	Archimedes, ch. 12A	A Young Macedonian, ch. 21, 22	Plutarch's Alexander, 8 pages
Geography	Visits to the Middle East, Visit 32				
Week 9, Lessons 161–165					
Bible	Esther; Ezra			Proverbs Study	Proverbs Study
History	Story of the Greeks, ch. 112–115	Our Little Athenian Cousin, ch. 13	Archimedes, ch. 12B	A Young Macedonian, ch. 23, 24	Plutarch's Alexander, 8 pages
Geography	Visits to the Middle East, Visit 33				
Week 10, Lessons 166–170					
Bible	Ezra; Nehemiah			Proverbs Study	Proverbs Study
History	Story of the Greeks, ch. 116–119	Our Little Athenian Cousin, ch. 14	Archimedes, ch. 13	A Young Macedonian, ch. 25, 26	Plutarch's Alexander, 8 pages
Geography	Visits to the Middle East, Visit 34				
Week 11, Lessons 171–175					
Bible	Nehemiah; Haggai; Zechariah; Malachi			Proverbs Study	Proverbs Study
History	Story of the Greeks, ch. 120–123	Our Little Athenian Cousin, ch. 15	Archimedes, ch. 14 and Appendix	A Young Macedonian, ch. 27, 28	Plutarch's Alexander, finish
Geography	Visits to the Middle East, Visit 35				
Week 12, Lessons 176–180					
Bible	Exam or Catch Up			Proverbs Study	Proverbs Study
History	Exam or Catch Up or Project	Our Little Athenian Cousin, ch. 16			
Geography	Visits to the Middle East, Visit 36				

Lesson 121: Joel

Materials Needed
- Bible
- *Wisdom for Life* (grades 7–12)

Family: Ask the students what they recall about how Joash became king. Explain that the prophet Joel lived during that time and had seen the wicked ways of Joash's grandmother, Athaliah, when she was queen. Joel's prophecy warns of a coming day of judgment and, later, God's deliverance for Judah. Read together Joel 1 and 2 and ask for an oral narration. Discuss what it means to "rend your hearts and not your garments" (Joel 2:13).

Grades 7–12: Continue working on *Wisdom for Life* Proverbs study.

Tip: As you cover the prophets throughout this Term, you will be reading portions of their books. You may want to have older students read through the entire prophetic books for truths to add to their Discovering Doctrine *notebooks.*

Lesson 122: Joash Repairs the Temple & Visit 25 to the Middle East

Materials Needed
- Bible
- Kings Chart; felt-tip markers
- *Visits to the Middle East*
- *Wisdom for Life* (grades 7–12)

Family: Ask students what they recall from last time's reading about the prophet Joel's message to Judah. Explain that young King Joash had an opportunity to help Judah return to the Lord; in today's reading students will discover what he did. Read together 2 Kings 12, 13, and 14. Ask the students to help you record the kings from today's reading in the appropriate columns on the chart and with the correct colors. Have them explain their choices.

Family: Complete Visit 25 in *Visits to the Middle East.*

Grades 7–12: Continue working on *Wisdom for Life* Proverbs study.

Lesson 123: Jonah

Materials Needed
- Bible

Book of Centuries Timeline

Joash becomes king of Judah (878 B.C.)

Book of Centuries Timeline

Jonah goes to Nineveh (c. 771 B.C.)

- *Then and Now Bible Maps*
- *Wisdom for Life* (grades 7–12)

Family: Explain that Assyria was the World Power at this time in history. The Assyrians were known as great and terrible conquerors, and most people would have thought that they deserved only punishment. Read together the book of Jonah and ask for an oral narration.

Look together at map 1 of Then and Now Bible Maps, Middle East - Bible Times, and ask the students to locate Nineveh. Place the map 2 overlay on top to discover which modern-day country Nineveh is in.

Tip: *Encourage older students to record any doctrinal truths from Jonah in their* Discovering Doctrine *books.*

Grades 7–12: Continue working on *Wisdom for Life* Proverbs study.

 Lesson 124: Death of Pelopidas

Materials Needed

- *The Story of the Greeks*
- *Archimedes and the Door of Science* (grades 4–6)
- *A Young Macedonian in the Army of Alexander the Great* (grades 7–9)
- *The Trial and Death of Socrates* (grades 10–12)

Family: Ask students what they recall about the two friends who saved Thebes from the Spartans: Pelopidas and Epaminondas. Read together *The Story of the Greeks*, chapters 82 and 83, "Death of Pelopidas" and "The Battle of Mantinea." Ask for an oral narration.

Grades 4–6: Read together or assign as independent reading *Archimedes and the Door of Science*, the first half of chapter 6, "Archimedes and Astronomy," pages 70–75. Ask for an oral or written narration.

Grades 7–9: Read together or assign as independent reading *A Young Macedonian in the Army of Alexander the Great*, chapter 7, "Memnon."

Grades 10–12: Read together or assign as independent reading *The Trial and Death of Socrates*, "Euthyphro." Ask for an oral or written narration.

Reminder: *Get* Plutarch's Lives *for lesson 134 for grades 10–12.*

 Lesson 125: The Tyrant of Syracuse

Materials Needed

- *The Story of the Greeks*

- *Then and Now Bible Maps*
- *Our Little Athenian Cousin of Long Ago* (grades 1–3 or 1–6)
- *A Young Macedonian in the Army of Alexander the Great* (grades 7–9)
- *The Trial and Death of Socrates* (grades 10–12)

Family: Locate the island of Sicily and its town of Syracuse on map 15, Paul's Journeys, in *Then and Now Bible Maps.* Explain that though this town had a cruel ruler, it had some excellent citizens from whom we can learn much. Read together *The Story of the Greeks*, chapters 84 and 85, "The Tyrant of Syracuse" and "Story of Damon and Pythias." Ask for an oral narration of what the students learned from the people they read about.

Grades 1–3 or 1–6: Read together *Our Little Athenian Cousin of Long Ago*, chapter 5, "At School."

Grades 7–9: Read together or assign as independent reading *A Young Macedonian in the Army of Alexander the Great,* chapter 8, "At Sea."

Grades 10–12: Read together or assign as independent reading *The Trial and Death of Socrates*, "Apology." Ask for an oral or written narration.

Tip: Make sure older children are up to date with their Discovering Doctrine *notebooks and their Book of Centuries entries.*

Book of Centuries Timeline

Lesson 126: Hosea

Materials Needed

- Bible
- *Wisdom for Life* (grades 7–12)

Family: Ask students what they recall from last time's reading about Jonah. Explain that today's reading is about another prophet who lived during that time. The message of his writings and his marriage to an unfaithful wife is a living picture: Israel was disloyal and unfaithful to the true God, yet God loved her and wanted to restore her. Read together Hosea 1, 3, and 14. Discuss how Israel was unfaithful to God and yet God loved her. Ask for an oral narration.

Tip: Encourage older students to read the rest of Hosea, looking for truths to add to Discovering Doctrine *if desired.*

Grades 7–12: Continue working on *Wisdom for Life* Proverbs study.

Book of Centuries Timeline

Lesson 127: Several More Kings & Visit 26 to the Middle East

Materials Needed

- Bible
- Kings Chart; felt-tip markers
- *Visits to the Middle East*
- *Wisdom for Life* (grades 7–12)

Family: Ask students what they recall from last time's reading about the prophet Hosea and his wife. Review your Kings Chart and look for any pattern in the colors. What trend can you see in the quality of kings for Judah? for Israel? Explain that today you will read about more kings and see if the trend continues. Read together 2 Kings 15 and 16. Ask the students to help you record the kings from today's reading in the appropriate columns on the chart and with the correct colors. Have them explain their choices.

Family: Complete Visit 26 in *Visits to the Middle East.*

Grades 7–12: Continue working on *Wisdom for Life* Proverbs study.

Lesson 128: Amos and Micah

Materials Needed

- Bible
- *Wisdom for Life* (grades 7–12)

Prophet Micah called (750 B.C.)

Family: Explain that Amos and Micah were also prophets who lived during the time of the Divided Kingdom. Both of them called the Israelites to turn from their sinful ways or experience a time of punishment from God. Read together Amos 5 and Micah 6 and ask students to listen for the reasons God would punish Israel and what He desired from them to show their repentance.

Tip: *Encourage older students to read the rest of Amos and Micah, looking for truths to add to* Discovering Doctrine *if desired.*

Grades 7–12: Continue working on *Wisdom for Life* Proverbs study.

Lesson 129: The Sword of Damocles

Materials Needed

- *The Story of the Greeks*

- *Archimedes and the Door of Science* (grades 4–6)
- *A Young Macedonian in the Army of Alexander the Great* (grades 7–9)
- *The Trial and Death of Socrates* (grades 10–12)

Family: Ask students what they recall from last time's reading about Dionysius, the tyrant of Syracuse on Sicily, and his interactions with Philoxenus and Damon and Pythias. Read together *The Story of the Greeks*, chapters 86 and 87, "The Sword of Damocles" and "Dion and Dionysius." Ask for an oral narration.

Grades 4–6: Read together or assign as independent reading *Archimedes and the Door of Science*, the last half of chapter 6, "Archimedes and Astronomy," pages 76–80. Ask for an oral or written narration.

Grades 7–9: Read together or assign as independent reading *A Young Macedonian in the Army of Alexander the Great*, chapter 9, "In Greece Again."

Grades 10–12: Read together or assign as independent reading *The Trial and Death of Socrates*, "Crito." Ask for an oral or written narration.

Lesson 130: Civil War in Syracuse

Materials Needed

- *The Story of the Greeks*
- *Our Little Athenian Cousin of Long Ago* (grades 1–3 or 1–6)
- *A Young Macedonian in the Army of Alexander the Great* (grades 7–9)
- *The Trial and Death of Socrates* (grades 10–12)

Family: Ask students what they recall from last time's reading about Dionysius the Younger's treatment of Plato. Explain that in today's reading they will find out what happened to the uncle, Dion, whom Dionysius had exiled. Read together *The Story of the Greeks*, chapters 88 and 89, "Civil War in Syracuse" and "Death of Dion." Ask for an oral narration.

Grades 1–3 or 1–6: Read together *Our Little Athenian Cousin of Long Ago*, chapter 6, "The Wrestling School."

Grades 7–9: Read together or assign as independent reading *A Young Macedonian in the Army of Alexander the Great*, chapter 10, "At Athens."

Grades 10–12: Read together or assign as independent reading *The Trial and Death of Socrates*, "Phaedo." Ask for an oral or written narration.

Book of Centuries Timeline

Book of Centuries Timeline

Lesson 131: The Fall of the Northern Kingdom

Materials Needed

- Bible
- Kings Chart; felt-tip markers
- *Then and Now Bible Maps*
- *Wisdom for Life* (grades 7–12)

Assyria conquers Israel and deports the people (721 B.C.)

Family: Look together at your Kings Chart to see the most recent king of Israel. (Pekah was killed by Hoshea.) Ask the students what they remember about his reign. Explain that today they will read about the last king of Israel during this time period and why he was the last one. Read together 2 Kings 17 and 18. Ask the students to help you record the kings from today's reading in the appropriate columns on the chart and with the correct colors. Have them explain their choices.

Look together at the map of the Assyrian Empire on map 4, Middle East, of Then and Now Bible Maps. The color code at the right illustrates how the empire expanded with successive rulers.

Grades 7–12: Continue working on *Wisdom for Life* Proverbs study.

Lesson 132: Isaiah & Visit 27 to the Middle East

Materials Needed

- Bible
- Kings Chart
- *Visits to the Middle East*
- *Wisdom for Life* (grades 7–12)

Family: Ask students what they recall from last time's reading about Israel's being conquered and carried away. Look at your Kings Chart and review what was happening in Judah during this time.

Explain that one of the prophets who lived during the reign of Hezekiah was Isaiah. His book is quite long and includes warnings to Judah and Jerusalem to repent, predictions of God's punishment for their sin, and promises of future restoration. A few historical accounts are included too. Read together Isaiah 1:1–20; 6:1–12; and 9:1–7. Ask for an oral narration after each passage. Encourage students to highlight any portions that they are familiar with.

***Tip:** Encourage older students to read the rest of Isaiah, looking for truths about God to add to* Discovering Doctrine *if desired. They may want to spread this reading over several days. If needed, direct attention specifically to chapter 40.*

Family: Complete Visit 27 in *Visits to the Middle East.*

Grades 7–12: Continue working on *Wisdom for Life* Proverbs study.

 Lesson 133: Hezekiah

Materials Needed

- Bible
- *The Stuff They Left Behind: From the Days of Ancient Greece*
- *Wisdom for Life* (grades 7–12)

Family: Ask students what they recall from last time's reading about Isaiah. Help them recall the events of 2 Kings 18 and explain that today they will find out what happened with King Hezekiah. Read together 2 Kings 19 and 20 and ask for an oral narration.

Display and discuss the picture of the Lachish Relief from The Stuff They Left Behind: From the Days of Ancient Greece portfolio.

Grades 7–12: Continue working on *Wisdom for Life* Proverbs study.

> ***Tip:** If your student has been reading Proverbs seven days a week, he should be ready to finish up the sixth topic and begin a new one this week. Assign a written narration that summarizes his findings if desired.*

 Lesson 134: Philip of Macedon

Materials Needed

- *The Story of the Greeks*
- *Archimedes and the Door of Science* (grades 4–6)
- *A Young Macedonian in the Army of Alexander the Great* (grades 7–9)
- *Plutarch's Lives* (grades 10–12)

Family: Look at the map on page 17 of *The Story of the Greeks* and find Macedonia. Explain that this country would become a strong force at this point in history. Read together *The Story of the Greeks*, chapters 90 and 91, "Philip of Macedon" and "Philip begins his Conquests." Ask for an oral narration.

Grades 4–6: Read together or assign as independent reading *Archimedes and the Door of Science*, chapter 7, "Archimedes and Mathematics." Ask for an oral or written narration.

Grades 7–9: Read together or assign as independent reading *A Young*

Book of Centuries Timeline

Sennacherib of Assyria attacks Jerusalem but does not overthrow it (713–710 B.C.)

Philip II reigns in Macedonia (360 B.C.)

Book of Centuries Timeline

Macedonian in the Army of Alexander the Great, chapter 11, "A Perilous Voyage."

Grades 10–12: Read together or assign as independent reading about four pages of Plutarch's biography of Alexander. Ask for an oral or written narration.

Lesson 135: The Orator Demosthenes

Materials Needed

- *The Story of the Greeks*
- *Our Little Athenian Cousin of Long Ago* (grades 1–3 or 1–6)
- *A Young Macedonian in the Army of Alexander the Great* (grades 7–9)
- *Plutarch's Lives* (grades 10–12)

Family: Ask students what they recall from last time's reading about Philip, king of Macedon. Read together *The Story of the Greeks*, chapters 92 and 93, "The Orator Demosthenes" and "Philip masters Greece." Ask for an oral narration.

Grades 1–3 or 1–6: Read together *Our Little Athenian Cousin of Long Ago*, chapter 7, "The Festival."

Grades 7–9: Read together or assign as independent reading *A Young Macedonian in the Army of Alexander the Great*, chapter 12, "On the Wrong Side."

Grades 10–12: Read together or assign as independent reading about four pages of Plutarch's biography of Alexander. Ask for an oral or written narration.

Tip: *Make sure older children are up to date with their* Discovering Doctrine *notebooks and their Book of Centuries entries.*

Lesson 136: Manasseh

Materials Needed

- Bible
- Kings Chart; felt-tip markers
- *Wisdom for Life* (grades 7–12)

Manasseh has the prophet Isaiah killed (c. 680 B.C.)

Family: Ask the students what they recall about King Hezekiah's death. Remind them that Hezekiah's son was Manasseh and explain that today's reading will be about his reign. Read together 2 Kings 21. Ask the students to help you record the kings from today's reading in the appropriate columns on the chart and with the correct colors. Have them explain their choices.

Grades 7–12: Continue working on *Wisdom for Life* Proverbs study.

Book of Centuries Timeline

Lesson 137: Nahum, Zephaniah, Habakkuk & Visit 28 to the Middle East

Materials Needed

- Bible
- *Visits to the Middle East*
- *Wisdom for Life* (grades 7–12)

Family: Write the three prophets' names—Nahum, Zephaniah, Habakkuk—on a sheet of paper or small white board. Display the prophets' names and tell students how to pronounce them.

Ask what the students remember about the prophet Jonah. Explain that more than 100 years after Jonah, Nineveh had returned to its idol worship and wicked ways. God directed the prophet Nahum to predict its destruction. Read together Nahum 1 and 2. Discuss the characteristics of God described in 1:2 and 3. He is jealous and avenging, yet slow to anger and uses His great power to punish the wicked.

Prophet Nahum called (668 B.C.)

Explain that just as Israel had been warned to repent, Zephaniah warned Judah to repent or experience God's punishment. Read together Zephaniah 1:1–13. Mention the phrase that is often repeated throughout these prophecies: the Day of the Lord. Ask students how that Day has been described in the prophets' messages.

Explain that the book of Habakkuk is written like a conversation with God. Habakkuk asked God two questions in his writings. If the students listen closely they will be able to identify the two questions and God's answer to each. Read together Habakkuk 1:1–11 and ask for an oral narration of the first question and answer. Then read together 1:12—2:20 and ask for the second question and answer. Finish with Habakkuk's song of praise and declaration of faith in 3:17–19.

Tip: *Encourage older students to read the rest of Nahum, Zephaniah, and Habakkuk, looking for truths to add to* Discovering Doctrine *if desired.*

Family: Complete Visit 28 in *Visits to the Middle East.*

Grades 7–12: Continue working on *Wisdom for Life* Proverbs study.

Book of Centuries Timeline

Lesson 138: Josiah

Materials Needed

- Bible
- Kings Chart; felt-tip markers
- *Wisdom for Life* (grades 7–12)

Josiah king of Judah (641–610 B.C.)

Family: Tell students that today's reading will be about a king of Judah who did what was right in the eyes of God. Ask students to guess how old that king was. Read together 2 Kings 22 and 23. Ask the students to help you record the kings from today's reading in the appropriate columns on the chart and with the correct colors. Have them explain their choices.

Grades 7–12: Continue working on *Wisdom for Life* Proverbs study.

Lesson 139: Birth of Alexander

Materials Needed

- *The Story of the Greeks*
- *Archimedes and the Door of Science* (grades 4–6)
- *A Young Macedonian in the Army of Alexander the Great* (grades 7–9)
- *Plutarch's Lives* (grades 10–12)

Birth of Alexander the Great (356 B.C.)

Family: Ask students what they recall from last time's reading about Philip of Macedon and his conquest of Greece. Explain that his son was ready to pick up where Philip left off. Read together *The Story of the Greeks*, chapters 94 and 95, "Birth of Alexander" and "The Steed Bucephalus." Ask for an oral narration.

Grades 4–6: Read together or assign as independent reading *Archimedes and the Door of Science*, chapter 8, "The Measurement of a Circle." Ask for an oral or written narration.

Grades 7–9: Read together or assign as independent reading *A Young Macedonian in the Army of Alexander the Great*, chapter 13, "Damascus."

Grades 10–12: Read together or assign as independent reading about four pages of Plutarch's biography of Alexander. Ask for an oral or written narration.

Lesson 140: Alexander as King

Materials Needed

- *The Story of the Greeks*

- *Our Little Athenian Cousin of Long Ago* (grades 1–3 or 1–6)
- *A Young Macedonian in the Army of Alexander the Great* (grades 7–9)
- *Plutarch's Lives* (grades 10–12)

Family: Ask students what they recall from last time's reading about Alexander's childhood. Read together *The Story of the Greeks*, chapters 96 and 97, "Alexander as King" and "Alexander and Diogenes." Ask for an oral narration.

Grades 1–3 or 1–6: Read together *Our Little Athenian Cousin of Long Ago*, chapter 8, "The Great Procession."

Grades 7–9: Read together or assign as independent reading *A Young Macedonian in the Army of Alexander the Great,* chapter 14, "Manasseh the Jew."

Grades 10–12: Read together or assign as independent reading about four pages of Plutarch's biography of Alexander. Ask for an oral or written narration.

Book of Centuries Timeline

Alexander begins to reign (336 B.C.)

Lesson 141: Jeremiah

Materials Needed

- Bible
- *Wisdom for Life* (grades 7–12)

Family: Ask students what they recall from last time's reading about King Josiah. Explain that Jeremiah began to prophesy during King Josiah's reign. He used some object lessons to illustrate and emphasize his prophecies. Read together these excerpts from Jeremiah and ask for oral narrations of the object lessons:

The Lesson of the Linen Belt (Girdle) in 13:1–11
The Lesson of the Potter in 18:1–12

Prophet Jeremiah called (629 B.C.)

Tip: Encourage older students to read the rest of Jeremiah, looking for truths to add to Discovering Doctrine *if desired. They may need to spread these readings over several days.*

Grades 7–12: Continue working on *Wisdom for Life* Proverbs study.

Lesson 142: The Fall of the Southern Kingdom & Visit 29 to the Middle East

Materials Needed

- Bible

Book of Centuries Timeline

- Kings Chart; felt-tip markers
- *Then and Now Bible Maps*
- *Visits to the Middle East*
- *Material World*
- *Wisdom for Life* (grades 7–12)

Nebuchadnezzar captures Judah (588 B.C.)

Family: Ask students what they recall from last time's reading of Jeremiah's prophecies. Explain that even the good kings and godly prophets were not enough to keep Judah from turning away from the Lord. Read together 2 Kings 24 and 25. Ask the students to help you record the kings from today's reading in the appropriate columns on the chart and with the correct colors. Have them explain their choices.

Look together at the Babylonian Kingdom map on page 4 of Then and Now Bible Maps and notice all the land that the Babylonians conquered during their reign as World Power (including Assyria, the former World Power).

Family: Complete Visit 29 in *Visits to the Middle East.*

Grades 7–12: Continue working on *Wisdom for Life* Proverbs study.

Lesson 143: Ezekiel and Lamentations

Materials Needed

- Bible
- *Wisdom for Life* (grades 7–12)

Family: Ask the students what they recall from last time's reading about Judah going into captivity. Explain that when Judah was taken into captivity, Jeremiah wrote Lamentations, which means "cries of sorrow and grief." Yet even in the midst of his sorrow, Jeremiah trusted the Lord. Read together Lamentations 3:1–26.

Write the name "Ezekiel" on a sheet of paper or small white board and post it. Explain that Ezekiel was another prophet who predicted Judah's destruction and future restoration. Read together Ezekiel 15 and 37:1–14 and ask for an oral narration after each passage.

> ***Tip:*** *Encourage older students to read the rest of Lamentations and Ezekiel, looking for truths to add to* Discovering Doctrine *if desired. They may need to spread these readings over several days.*

Grades 7–12: Continue working on *Wisdom for Life* Proverbs study.

Lesson 144: Alexander's Brilliant Beginning

Materials Needed

- *The Story of the Greeks*

Book of Centuries Timeline

- *Archimedes and the Door of Science* (grades 4–6)
- *A Young Macedonian in the Army of Alexander the Great* (grades 7–9)
- *Plutarch's Lives* (grades 10–12)

Family: Ask students what they recall from last time's reading about how Alexander reclaimed Macedonia's rule over the Greek states and met Diogenes the cynic. Read together *The Story of the Greeks*, chapters 98 and 99, "Alexander's Brilliant Beginning" and "The Gordian Knot." Ask for an oral narration.

Grades 4–6: Read together or assign as independent reading *Archimedes and the Door of Science*, chapter 9, "Archimedes and Numbers." Ask for an oral or written narration.

Grades 7–9: Read together or assign as independent reading *A Young Macedonian in the Army of Alexander the Great*, chapter 15, "Andromache."

Grades 10–12: Read together or assign as independent reading about four pages of Plutarch's biography of Alexander. Ask for an oral or written narration.

 Lesson 145: Alexander's Royal Captives

Materials Needed
- *The Story of the Greeks*
- *The Stuff They Left Behind: From the Days of Ancient Greece*
- *Our Little Athenian Cousin of Long Ago* (grades 1–3 or 1–6)
- *A Young Macedonian in the Army of Alexander the Great* (grades 7–9)
- *Plutarch's Lives* (grades 10–12)

Family: Ask students what they recall from last time's reading about Alexander's brilliant beginning. Display and discuss the picture of the Mosaic of Alexander the Great from *The Stuff They Left Behind: From the Days of Ancient Greece* portfolio.

Explain that in today's reading, Alexander met Darius in battle. Read together *The Story of the Greeks*, chapters 100 and 101, "Alexander's Royal Captives" and "Alexander at Jerusalem." Ask for an oral narration. Read Daniel 8 as desired.

Grades 1–3 or 1–6: Read together *Our Little Athenian Cousin of Long Ago*, chapter 9, "Hiero's Uncle is Ill."

Grades 7–9: Read together or assign as independent reading *A Young Macedonian in the Army of Alexander the Great,* chapter 16, "To Jerusalem."

Grades 10–12: Read together or assign as independent reading about four pages of Plutarch's biography of Alexander. Ask for an oral or written narration.

Book of Centuries Timeline

Tip: Make sure older children are up to date with their Discovering Doctrine *notebooks and their Book of Centuries entries.*

Lesson 146: Daniel in Babylon

Daniel taken captive to Babylon (607 B.C.)

Materials Needed

- Bible
- *Wisdom for Life* (grades 7–12)

Family: Ask the students what they recall about Judah's destruction and captivity. Explain that one young man who was taken captive by King Nebuchadnezzar left a record of his experience. Today's reading will be about him. Read together Daniel 1 and 2 and ask for an oral narration.

Grades 7–12: Continue working on *Wisdom for Life* Proverbs study.

Lesson 147: The Fiery Furnace & Visit 30 to the Middle East

Materials Needed

- Bible
- *Visits to the Middle East*
- *Wisdom for Life* (grades 7–12)

Family: Ask students what they recall from last time's reading about Daniel's initial years in Babylon. Read together Daniel 3 and ask for an oral narration.

Family: Complete Visit 30 in *Visits to the Middle East.*

Grades 7–12: Continue working on *Wisdom for Life* Proverbs study.

Lesson 148: Nebuchadnezzar's Letter

Materials Needed

- Bible
- *The Stuff They Left Behind: From the Days of Ancient Greece*
- *Wisdom for Life* (grades 7–12)

Family: Ask the students what they recall about King Nebuchadnezzar from previous readings. Display and discuss the picture of the Ishtar Gate from *The Stuff They Left Behind: From the Days of Ancient Greece* portfolio.

Explain that today's Bible reading is a letter that Nebuchadnezzar wrote. It describes how God got his attention. Read together Daniel 4 and ask for an oral narration.

Grades 7–12: Continue working on *Wisdom for Life* Proverbs study.

Book of Centuries Timeline

Lesson 149: The African Desert

Materials Needed

- *The Story of the Greeks*
- *Archimedes and the Door of Science* (grades 4–6)
- *A Young Macedonian in the Army of Alexander the Great* (grades 7–9)
- *Plutarch's Lives* (grades 10–12)

Family: Ask students what they recall from last time's reading about how Alexander treated Darius' family and about Alexander in Jerusalem. Trace his route so far on the map on page 18 and see where he went after Jerusalem. Read together *The Story of the Greeks*, chapters 102 and 103, "The African Desert" and "Death of Darius." Ask for an oral narration.

Grades 4–6: Read together or assign as independent reading *Archimedes and the Door of Science*, chapter 10, "Archimedes and the Centers of Gravity." Ask for an oral or written narration.

Grades 7–9: Read together or assign as independent reading *A Young Macedonian in the Army of Alexander the Great*, chapter 17, "Tyre."

Grades 10–12: Read together or assign as independent reading about four pages of Plutarch's biography of Alexander. Ask for an oral or written narration.

Lesson 150: Defeat of Porus

Materials Needed

- *The Story of the Greeks*
- *Our Little Athenian Cousin of Long Ago* (grades 1–3 or 1–6)
- *A Young Macedonian in the Army of Alexander the Great* (grades 7–9)
- *Plutarch's Lives* (grades 10–12)

Family: Ask students what they recall about Alexander's trek across the African desert, time in Babylon, and final meeting with Darius. Read together *The Story of the Greeks*, chapters 104 and 105, "Defeat of Porus" and "The Return to Babylon," following his route on the map on page 18. Ask for an oral narration.

Grades 1–3 or 1–6: Read together *Our Little Athenian Cousin of Long Ago*, chapter 10, "Festival of the Bear."

Grades 7–9: Read together or assign as independent reading *A Young Macedonian in the Army of Alexander the Great*, chapter 18, "The Escape."

Book of Centuries Timeline

Grades 10–12: Read together or assign as independent reading about four pages of Plutarch's biography of Alexander. Ask for an oral or written narration.

Lesson 151: The Writing on the Wall

Materials Needed

- Bible
- *Then and Now Bible Maps*
- *Wisdom for Life* (grades 7–12)

Belshazzar's feast (538 B.C.)

Family: Ask students what they recall about Daniel's time in Babylon so far. Explain that the next account Daniel wrote about was after King Nebuchadnezzar had died and his son, Belshazzar, was reigning.

Look together at map 4 in *Then and Now Bible Maps*. Notice how the Babylonian Kingdom was swallowed up by the Kingdoms of the Medes and Persians.

Explain that when the events of Daniel 5 took place, Babylon had been under a siege for quite a while already. The Mede and Persian army was on its doorstep. Read together Daniel 5 and ask for an oral narration.

Grades 7–12: Assign as independent reading Daniel 7 and 8, which are a record of prophecies Daniel had during King Belshazzar's reign. Have students narrate both prophecies and their interpretations.

Continue working on *Wisdom for Life* Proverbs study.

***Tip:** If your student has been reading Proverbs five days a week, he should be ready to finish up the fifth topic and begin a new one this week. Assign a written narration that summarizes his findings if desired.*

Lesson 152: Daniel in the Lions' Den & Visit 31 to the Middle East

Materials Needed

- Bible
- *The Stuff They Left Behind: From the Days of Ancient Greece*
- *Visits to the Middle East*
- *Hungry Planet: What the World Eats*
- *Wisdom for Life* (grades 7–12)

Family: Ask students what they recall from last time's reading about how the Medes and the Persians conquered Babylon. Display and discuss the picture of the Medes and Persians Relief from *The Stuff They Left Behind: From* the *Days of Ancient Greece* portfolio.

Explain that when the Mede and Persian army conquered Babylon, a new king took over: King Darius. Read together Daniel 6 and ask for an oral narration.

Tip: Encourage older students to read the rest of Daniel, looking for truths to add to Discovering Doctrine *if desired.*

Family: Complete Visit 31 in *Visits to the Middle East.*

Grades 7–12: Continue working on *Wisdom for Life* Proverbs study.

Book of Centuries Timeline

Lesson 153: The First Exiles Return to Jerusalem

Materials Needed
- Bible
- *Then and Now Bible Maps*
- *Wisdom for Life* (grades 7–12)

Family: Ask the students what they recall about Jeremiah's prophecies. Read together Jeremiah 29:10–14 and explain that today they will read how Jeremiah's prophecy came true. Read together Ezra 1:1—2:1 and chapter 3 and ask for an oral narration.

Cyrus allows the Jews to return to Jerusalem to rebuild the temple (537 B.C.)

Look together at the Persian Empire on map 4 in *Then and Now Bible Maps*. Ask the students to find Babylon and Jerusalem and to consider why some of the Jews who were in Babylon might have decided not to make the journey to return to Jerusalem. (Map 1 gives a closer view with a mileage key.)

Grades 7–12: Continue working on *Wisdom for Life* Proverbs study.

Lesson 154: Death of Alexander the Great

Materials Needed
- *The Story of the Greeks*
- *Archimedes and the Door of Science* (grades 4–6)
- *A Young Macedonian in the Army of Alexander the Great* (grades 7–9)
- *Plutarch's Lives* (grades 10–12)

Family: Ask students what they recall from last time's reading about Alexander's further travels. Read together *The Story of the Greeks*, chapters 106 and 107, "Death of Alexander the Great" and "The Division of the Realm." Ask for an oral narration.

Death of Alexander (323 B.C.)

Book of Centuries Timeline

Grades 4–6: Read together or assign as independent reading *Archimedes and the Door of Science*, chapter 11, "The Sphere and the Cylinder." Ask for an oral or written narration.

Grades 7–9: Read together or assign as independent reading *A Young Macedonian in the Army of Alexander the Great*, chapter 19, "The High Priest."

Grades 10–12: Read together or assign as independent reading about four pages of Plutarch's biography of Alexander. Ask for an oral or written narration.

Lesson 155: Death of Demosthenes

Materials Needed

- *The Story of the Greeks*
- *Our Little Athenian Cousin of Long Ago* (grades 1–3 or 1–6)
- *A Young Macedonian in the Army of Alexander the Great* (grades 7–9)
- *Plutarch's Lives* (grades 10–12)

Alexander's generals battle over his empire; Euclid, Archimedes (323–276 B.C.)

Family: Ask students what they recall from last time's reading about Alexander's death and what happened to his empire afterward. Remind students that all this time there had been a man in Athens who spoke eloquently against Alexander: Demosthenes. Ask students what they recall about Demosthenes. Read together *The Story of the Greeks*, chapters 108 and 109, "Death of Demosthenes" and "The Last of the Athenians." Ask for an oral narration.

Grades 1–3 or 1–6: Read together *Our Little Athenian Cousin of Long Ago*, chapter 11, "The New Slave."

Grades 7–9: Read together or assign as independent reading *A Young Macedonian in the Army of Alexander the Great,* chapter 20, "From Tyre to the Tigris."

Grades 10–12: Read together or assign as independent reading about four pages of Plutarch's biography of Alexander. Ask for an oral or written narration.

Tip: Make sure older children are up to date with their Discovering Doctrine *notebooks and their Book of Centuries entries.*

Lesson 156: Darius' Decree

Materials Needed

- Bible
- *Wisdom for Life* (grades 7–12)

Family: Ask the students what they recall from last time's reading about the Israelites' returning to Jerusalem from Babylon. Explain that not everyone was happy about their rebuilding their homeland. Read together Ezra 4—6 and ask for an oral narration.

Grades 7–12: Continue working on *Wisdom for Life* Proverbs study.

Book of Centuries Timeline

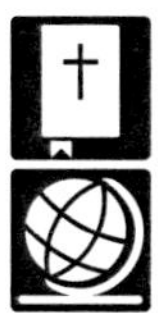

Lesson 157: Esther Becomes Queen & Visit 32 to the Middle East

Materials Needed

- Bible
- *Visits to the Middle East*
- *Wisdom for Life* (grades 7–12)

Family: Explain that while some Jews had returned to Jerusalem, others had stayed behind in Persia (formerly Babylon). At one point they were in danger of being massacred, and today's reading will start that story. Read together Esther 1 and 2 and ask for an oral narration.

Family: Complete Visit 32 in *Visits to the Middle East.*

Grades 7–12: Continue working on *Wisdom for Life* Proverbs study.

Tip: If your student has been reading Proverbs seven days a week, he should be ready to finish up the seventh topic and begin the final one this week. Assign a written narration that summarizes his findings if desired.

Lesson 158: Wicked Haman's Plot

Materials Needed

- Bible
- *Wisdom for Life* (grades 7–12)

Family: Ask students what they recall from last time's reading about Esther and Mordecai. Read together Esther 3 and 4 and ask for an oral narration.

Grades 7–12: Continue working on *Wisdom for Life* Proverbs study.

Book of Centuries Timeline

Ptolemy enslaves Judea by subterfuge (320 B.C.)

Lesson 159: Ptolemy in Judea

Materials Needed

- *The Story of the Greeks*
- *Archimedes and the Door of Science* (grades 4–6)
- *A Young Macedonian in the Army of Alexander the Great* (grades 7–9)
- *Plutarch's Lives* (grades 10–12)

Family: Ask students what they recall from last time's reading about the intrigues and final outcome of Alexander's generals, family, and empire. Read together *The Story of the Greeks*, chapter 110, "Ptolemy in Judea." Ask for an oral narration.

Discuss the sequence of the events being read about in Bible lessons and history lessons. Use the Book of Centuries dates to show the chronological order of the Jews' return from Babylon, Esther's saving the Jews from slaughter, Alexander the Great's visit to Jerusalem, and Ptolemy's conquest of Judea.

Grades 4–6: Read together or assign as independent reading *Archimedes and the Door of Science*, the first half of chapter 12, "The War Machines of Archimedes," pages 110–116. Ask for an oral or written narration.

Grades 7–9: Read together or assign as independent reading *A Young Macedonian in the Army of Alexander the Great*, chapter 21, "Arbela."

Grades 10–12: Read together or assign as independent reading about four pages of Plutarch's biography of Alexander. Ask for an oral or written narration.

Lesson 160: The Wonderful Library

Materials Needed

- *The Story of the Greeks*
- *Our Little Athenian Cousin of Long Ago* (grades 1–3 or 1–6)
- *A Young Macedonian in the Army of Alexander the Great* (grades 7–9)
- *Plutarch's Lives* (grades 10–12)

Family: Ask students what they recall from last time's reading about how Ptolemy gained Judea by subterfuge. Read together *The Story of the Greeks*, chapter 111, "The Wonderful Library." Ask for an oral narration.

Grades 1–3 or 1–6: Read together *Our Little Athenian Cousin of Long Ago*, chapter 12, "Preparing to Be Soldiers."

Grades 7–9: Read together or assign as independent reading *A Young Macedonian in the Army of Alexander the Great,* chapter 22, "At Babylon."

Grades 10–12: Read together or assign as independent reading about four pages of Plutarch's biography of Alexander. Ask for an oral or written narration.

Book of Centuries Timeline

 Lesson 161: Esther's Request

Materials Needed

- Bible
- *Wisdom for Life* (grades 7–12)

Family: Ask the students what they recall from last time's reading about Haman's plot to destroy the Jews in Persia. Read together Esther 5—7 and ask for an oral narration.

Esther saves her people (510 B.C.)

Grades 7–12: Continue working on *Wisdom for Life* Proverbs study.

 Lesson 162: The Jews Triumph & Visit 33 to the Middle East

Materials Needed

- Bible
- *Visits to the Middle East*
- *Wisdom for Life* (grades 7–12)

Family: Ask students what they recall from last time's reading about Esther's efforts to save her people. Read together Esther 8—10 and ask for an oral narration.

Family: Complete Visit 33 in *Visits to the Middle East.*

Grades 7–12: Continue working on *Wisdom for Life* Proverbs study.

 Lesson 163: Ezra Returns to Jerusalem

Materials Needed

- Bible
- *Wisdom for Life* (grades 7–12)

Family: Ask the students what they recall about the Jews who had returned to Jerusalem and were trying to rebuild there. Explain that God once again moved a king's heart to help them. Read together Ezra 7 and 8:15-36 and ask for an oral narration.

Grades 7–12: Continue working on *Wisdom for Life* Proverbs study.

Book of Centuries Timeline

Lesson 164: The Colossus of Rhodes

Materials Needed

- *The Story of the Greeks*
- *Archimedes and the Door of Science* (grades 4–6)
- *A Young Macedonian in the Army of Alexander the Great* (grades 7–9)
- *Plutarch's Lives* (grades 10–12)

Colossus of Rhodes built (290 B.C.)

Family: Ask students what they recall from last time's reading about the wonderful library at Alexandria. Review what Alexander's generals' attitudes were toward the empire and each other, and ask students what they think happened next. Read together *The Story of the Greeks*, chapters 112 and 113, "The Colossus of Rhodes" and "The Battle of Ipsus." Ask for an oral narration.

Grades 4–6: Read together or assign as independent reading *Archimedes and the Door of Science*, the last half of chapter 12, "The War Machines of Archimedes," pages 117–123. Ask for an oral or written narration.

Grades 7–9: Read together or assign as independent reading *A Young Macedonian in the Army of Alexander the Great*, chapter 23, "A Glimpse into the Future."

***Tip:** Chapter 23 contains a scene in which the two chief characters of the story visit a Babylonian magician. The fortune-telling scene is brief and accompanied by the characters' doubts about its authenticity. A valuable look at what was a stronghold in that culture but approached with healthy skepticism and balance.*

Grades 10–12: Read together or assign as independent reading about four pages of Plutarch's biography of Alexander. Ask for an oral or written narration.

Lesson 165: Demetrius and the Athenians

Materials Needed

- *The Story of the Greeks*
- *Our Little Athenian Cousin of Long Ago* (grades 1–3 or 1–6)
- *A Young Macedonian in the Army of Alexander the Great* (grades 7–9)
- *Plutarch's Lives* (grades 10–12)

Septuagint translation of the Scriptures made in Alexandria (277 B.C.)

Family: Ask students what they recall from last time's reading about Demetrius and the Athenians' changing attitudes toward him. Read together *The Story of the Greeks*, chapters 114 and 115, "Demetrius and the Athenians" and "The Achaean League." Ask for an oral narration.

Grades 1–3 or 1–6: Read together *Our Little Athenian Cousin of Long Ago*, chapter 13, "A Story in the Studio."

Grades 7–9: Read together or assign as independent reading *A Young Macedonian in the Army of Alexander the Great,* chapter 24, "Vengeance."

Grades 10–12: Read together or assign as independent reading about four pages of Plutarch's biography of Alexander. Ask for an oral or written narration.

Tip: Make sure older children are up to date with their Discovering Doctrine *notebooks and their Book of Centuries entries.*

Lesson 166: The People Obey God

Materials Needed

- Bible
- *Wisdom for Life* (grades 7–12)

Family: Ask the students what they remember from last time's reading about Ezra's return to Jerusalem. Read together Ezra 9 and 10:1–17 and ask for an oral narration.

Grades 7–12: Continue working on *Wisdom for Life* Proverbs study.

Lesson 167: Nehemiah Comes to Jerusalem & Visit 34 to the Middle East

Materials Needed

- Bible
- *Then and Now Bible Maps*
- *Visits to the Middle East*
- *Wisdom for Life* (grades 7–12)

Family: Ask students what they recall from last time's reading about the Israelites' response to God's Law when Ezra read it. Explain that God rose up another leader to help with rebuilding Jerusalem. Read together Nehemiah 1 and 2 and ask for an oral narration.

Look together at the Persian Empire on map 4 in *Then and Now Bible Maps* and determine where Nehemiah was when he got the word about Jerusalem.

Family: Complete Visit 34 in *Visits to the Middle East.*

Grades 7–12: Continue working on *Wisdom for Life* Proverbs study.

Book of Centuries Timeline

Ezra leads the second major wave of returning Jews (c. 467 B.C.)

Nehemiah rebuilds the walls of Jerusalem (c. 454 B.C.)

Book of Centuries Timeline

Lesson 168: The Walls Rebuilt

Materials Needed

- Bible
- *Wisdom for Life* (grades 7–12)

Family: Ask students what they recall from last time's reading about Nehemiah's desire to rebuild the walls of Jerusalem. Explain that he organized the people and assigned them various sections of the wall to work on. Read together Nehemiah 4—6 and ask for an oral narration.

Grades 7–12: Continue working on *Wisdom for Life* Proverbs study.

Lesson 169: Division in Sparta

Materials Needed

- *The Story of the Greeks*
- *Archimedes and the Door of Science* (grades 4–6)
- *A Young Macedonian in the Army of Alexander the Great* (grades 7–9)
- *Plutarch's Lives* (grades 10–12)

Family: Ask students what they recall from last time's reading about the Achaean League. Ask students what they think had been happening in Sparta during all this time. Read together *The Story of the Greeks*, chapters 116 and 117, "Division in Sparta" and "Death of Agis." Ask for an oral narration.

Grades 4–6: Read together or assign as independent reading *Archimedes and the Door of Science*, chapter 13, "The End of Archimedes." Ask for an oral or written narration.

Grades 7–9: Read together or assign as independent reading *A Young Macedonian in the Army of Alexander the Great*, chapter 25, "Darius."

Grades 10–12: Read together or assign as independent reading about four pages of Plutarch's biography of Alexander. Ask for an oral or written narration.

Lesson 170: The War of the Two Leagues

Materials Needed

- *The Story of the Greeks*
- *Our Little Athenian Cousin of Long Ago* (grades 1–3 or 1–6)
- *A Young Macedonian in the Army of Alexander the Great* (grades 7–9)
- *Plutarch's Lives* (grades 10–12)

Family: Ask students what they recall from last time's reading about the divisions in Sparta and King Agis. Read together *The Story of the Greeks,* chapters 118 and 119, "The War of the Two Leagues" and "The Last of the Greeks." Ask for an oral narration.

Grades 1–3 or 1–6: Read together *Our Little Athenian Cousin of Long Ago,* chapter 14, "Duris Leaves Athens."

Grades 7–9: Read together or assign as independent reading *A Young Macedonian in the Army of Alexander the Great,* chapter 26, "Invalided."

Grades 10–12: Read together or assign as independent reading about four pages of Plutarch's biography of Alexander. Ask for an oral or written narration.

Reminder: *If you want to do an optional hands-on project for lesson 179 or 180, start collecting the materials you will need.*

Book of Centuries Timeline

Sparta makes a treaty with Rome (211 B.C.)

Lesson 171: Confession and Celebration

Materials Needed

- Bible
- *Wisdom for Life* (grades 7–12)

Family: Ask the students what they remember from last time's reading about Nehemiah and his project. Explain that once the walls were finished, Nehemiah and Ezra took steps to encourage the people to continue in God's ways. Read together Nehemiah 8, 9, and 13 and ask for an oral narration.

Grades 7–12: Continue working on *Wisdom for Life* Proverbs study.

Lesson 172: Haggai and Zechariah & Visit 35 to the Middle East

Materials Needed

- Bible
- *Visits to the Middle East*
- *Wisdom for Life* (grades 7–12)

Family: Ask the students to name as many prophets as they can remember. Explain that there were prophets after the people returned from captivity too. These prophets encouraged the people to remain true to God and obey Him. Write these names on a sheet of paper or small white board and display them: "Haggai" and "Zechariah."

Book of Centuries Timeline

Explain that the people who returned to the Promised Land had neglected to rebuild the Temple; instead, they had turned their attention to their own crops and houses. Haggai rebuked them for their self-centeredness and revealed how God was not blessing their efforts because they were not putting Him first. Read together the book of Haggai and ask for an oral narration.

Zechariah prophesied while they were building the Temple and afterwards. Read Zechariah 1:1–6. Discuss why the Israelites needed these constant reminders to follow God. Are believers today different from or similar to those Israelites? Why?

Tip: Encourage older students to read the rest of Haggai and Zechariah, looking for truths to add to Discovering Doctrine *if desired.*

Family: Complete Visit 35 in *Visits to the Middle East.*

Grades 7–12: Continue working on *Wisdom for Life* Proverbs study.

Lesson 173: Malachi

Materials Needed

- Bible
- *Wisdom for Life* (grades 7–12)

Prophet Malachi (416 B.C.)

Family: Write the name "Malachi" on a sheet of paper or small white board and display it for students to see. Explain that Malachi was the last Old Testament prophet. Though the Jews had returned to their homeland and worship at the Temple had been reinstituted, many of them were still living like the Babylonians and Persians did. They were neglecting God's laws—even the priests. Malachi pointed out how they were sinning. Read together the book of Malachi and discuss how the people were sinning and any lessons from them we can learn for our lives today.

Tip: Encourage older students to record any doctrinal truths from Malachi in their Discovering Doctrine *books.*

Grades 7–12: Continue working on *Wisdom for Life* Proverbs study.

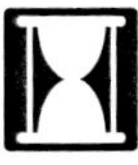

Lesson 174: Ptolemy and Antiochus at Jerusalem

Materials Needed

- *The Story of the Greeks*
- *Archimedes and the Door of Science* (grades 4–6)

- *A Young Macedonian in the Army of Alexander the Great* (grades 7–9)
- *Plutarch's Lives* (grades 10–12)

Family: Ask students what they recall from last time's reading about Malachi. Explain that the events in today's reading took place about 200 years after the prophet Malachi. Read together *The Story of the Greeks*, chapters 120 and 121, "Ptolemy and Antiochus at Jerusalem" and "The Abomination of Desolation." Ask for an oral narration.

Grades 4–6: Read together or assign as independent reading *Archimedes and the Door of Science*, chapter 14, "No End to Archimedes," and the Appendix, "Archimedes' Writings." Ask for an oral or written narration.

Grades 7–9: Read together or assign as independent reading *A Young Macedonian in the Army of Alexander the Great*, chapter 27, "News from the East."

Grades 10–12: Read together or assign as independent reading about four pages of Plutarch's biography of Alexander. Ask for an oral or written narration.

Lesson 175: The Victorious Jews

Materials Needed

- *The Story of the Greeks*
- *Our Little Athenian Cousin of Long Ago* (grades 1–3 or 1–6)
- *A Young Macedonian in the Army of Alexander the Great* (grades 7–9)
- *Plutarch's Lives* (grades 10–12)

Family: Ask students what they recall from last time's reading about Antiochus' treatment of the Jews in Judea and Mattathias' resistance. Read together *The Story of the Greeks*, chapters 122 and 123, "The Victorious Jews" and "Greece a Roman Province." Ask for an oral narration.

Grades 1–3 or 1–6: Read together *Our Little Athenian Cousin of Long Ago*, chapter 15, "The Beginning of War."

Grades 7–9: Read together or assign as independent reading *A Young Macedonian in the Army of Alexander the Great*, chapter 28, "The End."

Grades 10–12: Read together or assign as independent reading the rest of Plutarch's biography of Alexander. Ask for an oral or written narration.

> ***Tip:*** *Make sure older children are up to date with their* Discovering Doctrine *notebooks and their Book of Centuries entries.*

Book of Centuries Timeline

Ptolemy attempts to desecrate the Jewish Temple (217 B.C.)

Maccabees retake Jerusalem and purify Temple (165 B.C.)

Rome conquers Corinth and makes Greece a Roman province (146 B.C.)

Book of Centuries Timeline

Lesson 176: Bible Catch Up or Exam

Materials Needed

- Bible (if doing catch-up reading)

Family: Use this day to catch up on any reading you need to finish, or use the question below for the students' exam.

Exam Question: Have students work all together to think of ten words that begin with the letter *C* that will summarize the main events of Joshua through Malachi. (For example, they might use "conquest" to summarize the book of Joshua or "chaos" for Judges.) List the ten words where all the students can see them.

Ask each student to select one or two words from the list and to tell all he or she can remember that is included in the selected summary word.

Tip: Students will be selecting and narrating from the rest of the words over the next two lessons. If you have many students, you may want to make sure you leave enough words for those future narrations, or you may just want to allow your students to complete this exam early. Either way is fine; it's your choice.

Grades 7–12: If older students have not yet written their narrations for the Proverbs studies they have done, you may want to use this week for them to catch up on that assignment.

Lesson 177: Bible Catch Up or Exam & Visit 36 to the Middle East

Materials Needed

- Bible (if doing catch-up reading)
- *Visits to the Middle East*

Family: Use this day to catch up on any reading you need to finish, or use the question below for the students' exam.

Exam Question: Ask each student to select one or two words from the remaining list of *C* words and to tell all he or she can remember that is included in the selected summary word.

Family: Complete Visit 36 in *Visits to the Middle East.*

Book of Centuries Timeline

Lesson 178: Bible Catch Up or Exam

Materials Needed
- Bible (if doing catch-up reading)

Family: Use this day to catch up on any reading you need to finish, or use the question below for the students' exam.

Exam Question: Ask each student to select one or two words from the remaining list of *C* words and to tell all he or she can remember that is included in the selected summary word.

__Tip:__ If your student has been reading Proverbs five days a week, he should be ready to finish up the sixth topic this week. Assign a written narration that summarizes his findings if desired.

Lesson 179: Ancient Greece Catch-Up, Project, or Exam

Materials Needed
- (optional) Materials for hands-on project

Family: Use this day to catch up on any reading you need to finish, or use the questions below for part of the students' exam on their Ancient Greece readings. An optional hands-on project is also given if you would prefer to do that instead.
Grades 1–3: Tell about life in Athens.
Grades 4–6: Tell all you know about Alexander the Great.
Grades 7–9: Explain what each of these expressions means today and tell the story behind it: "A sword is hanging over his head" and "He has cut the Gordian knot."
Grades 10–12: Trace the changing relationship of the Israelites to the countries around them (Assyria, Egypt, Babylon, Persia, Greece), explain what caused those changes, and describe what effects those changes had. Cite examples from your reading.

Optional Hands-On Project: Select a hands-on project from the Links and Tips page: http://simplycm.com/joshua-links

Lesson 180: Ancient Greece Catch-Up, Project, or Exam

Materials Needed
- *Our Little Athenian Cousin of Long Ago* (grades 1–3 or 1–6)

Book of Centuries Timeline

• (optional) Materials for hands-on project

Family: Use this day to catch up on any reading you need to finish, or use the questions below for the rest of the students' exam on their Ancient Greece readings. An optional hands-on project is also given if you would prefer to do that instead.
Grades 1–3: Tell a story from Alexander the Great's life.
Grades 4–6: Tell fully about Archimedes—the person and his accomplishments.
Grades 7–9: Describe the events that led to the fall of Greece as a world power.
Grades 10–12: From your readings on Ancient Greece, draw out three people whom you would consider great—in either power or character—and explain fully what made each one great.

Optional Hands-On Project: Complete your hands-on project or select a new one from the Links and Tips page: http://simplycm.com/joshua-links

Grades 1–3 or 1–6: Read together *Our Little Athenian Cousin of Long Ago*, chapter 16, "Hiero the Victor."

> ***Tip:*** *If your student has been reading Proverbs seven days a week, he should be ready to finish up the final topic. Assign a written narration that summarizes his findings if desired. Students who have been reading Proverbs five days a week may continue the study and finish all the topics if desired.*

Helpful Information

Why I Wrote These Lessons

When I was growing up in Sunday School and church, I heard the stories of the Bible many times. I could tell you all the details of Who, What, Why, and How. But I never thought about the When. I knew those Bible accounts were true, just like the history accounts I read were true, but I never put the two subjects together to comprehend how Bible events fit into world history events.

I also never thought about how the different Bible stories fit together. For example, I knew the story of Joseph's being sold into slavery and eventually rising into the place of leadership in Egypt, and I knew the story of Moses and the Exodus, but I never connected the two mentally as a sort of cause and effect until I studied them with my children in chronological order. Suddenly all the pieces started fitting together!

After that experience, I knew how I wanted to teach my children the Bible: in chronological order alongside world history—and I wanted to make the Bible history most important. Charlotte Mason emphasized the priority Bible lessons should have in our curriculum: "Their Bible lessons should help them to realise in early days that the knowledge of God is the principal knowledge, and, therefore, that their Bible lessons are their chief lessons" (Vol. 1, p. 251). As our children study Bible accounts intertwined with world history, they learn to see God's hand of sovereignty moving in the events. They come to know God's character through His Word and begin to interpret world happenings through a Biblical worldview. They absorb God's truth and can discern and refute false beliefs that man has embraced throughout history.

So the lessons in this book will walk you through Scripture passages to read, living books to use, and optional hands-on activities to do as you continue working your way through the Bible—from Joshua through Malachi, including Ancient Greece. You'll also find narration ideas, teaching tips, and Book of Centuries dates to help you see how the Bible accounts fit into world history events.

One of my main goals is to show you how you can teach the same historical time period to all of your children at the same time, no matter what grades they are in. I firmly believe in the advantages that a one-room schoolhouse approach can bring. You will save time in both planning and teaching, and your children will grow together in community as they learn together and help each other.

Please keep in mind that this study is just a collection of suggestions. I'm simply passing along these suggestions to, hopefully, save you some time and give you some ideas. You know your children much better than I do, so feel free to change, add, or omit as you see fit. Remember, I used the books that were available to me; they may not be available to you. Don't be afraid to substitute.

Most of all, encourage the older children to help the younger, and allow the younger to look over the shoulder of the older; and together, enjoy these family studies of God's Word and history.

Charlotte Mason Methods Used in This Study

Living Books

Probably the most well known of Charlotte Mason's methods is her use of living books instead of dry, factual textbooks. Living books are usually written by one person who has a passion for the subject and writes in conversational or narrative style. The books pull you into the subject and involve your emotions, so it's easy to remember the events and facts. Living books make the subject "come alive." The books used in this study are living books. If you make a substitution, please do your best to select a living book.

Bible Readings: The Bible is the best living book! And Charlotte encouraged us to give our children plenty of direct contact with the Bible itself, not feed them just watered down retellings. So you will find throughout the lessons, the Scripture passages to read aloud directly from the Bible.

Now, Charlotte also recommended that we should omit those portions not "suitable" for children under the age of nine (Vol. 1, p. 248; Vol. 3, p. 330). I interpret "unsuitable" to mean those instances that are graphic or sexual in nature. So I have made note of some lessons that can be skipped for the younger children. But in those instances where the plot of the account is important for continuity in the study, I have recommended reading the account from *The Child's Story Bible* by Catherine Vos. Of all the children's story Bibles I have seen, this is one of the best. It stays very true to Scripture and includes many details and stories that most story Bibles omit. Catherine Vos also does a wonderful job of dealing in a tactful yet truthful way with passages that could potentially be unsuitable for younger children.

Narration

When you ask a child to narrate, you're asking him to tell back in his own words what he just saw, heard, or read. The narration can be oral or written or drawn—whatever. Because the child must think through the information and determine how to present it, mixed with his own opinion and impressions, this method of evaluation requires a much higher thinking level than mere fill-in-the-blank or answer-the-posed-question-with-a-fact methods. When requesting a child to narrate, word the question in an open, essay-type form, such as "Tell all you know about ___" or "Describe ___."

Oral Narration with Many Children: Usually it's good to start with the youngest child, then work your way up the ages asking if each has anything to add. However, if you use this approach every single time, the older ones might get complacent. ("No, nothing to add.") So you can mix things up a little by calling on any child at random to start the narration sometimes. Not knowing who will be selected to give the oral narration keeps everybody alert and listening. The key is to have one child start the narration and then have the others add to it, not repeat it. That mental exercise of remembering what was already mentioned and searching through your mind for something new to talk about is also a plus!

Written Narration: Older children can be expected to take the next step and write their narrations. If your older child is not used to doing narration, give him several weeks or months to get used to the idea and have some practice narrating orally first. It's harder to keep your train of thought when you have to also think about the mechanics of writing, punctuating, capitalizing, and all such trappings, so make sure your child is adept and successful with organizing and expressing his thoughts orally before adding the writing aspect. Once he is an "old pro" at oral narrations, you can ease him into the written narrations by requiring just one a week or so to begin with. The lessons in this book will give suggestions for some written narrations. You can determine which of your students can handle those assignments.

Also keep in mind that you can do narration in many ways. Oral is the quickest and simplest. But if you would like to keep things fresh, you can have the children express what they learned in various ways. We have a list of narration ideas on our website that might help you: http://simplycm.com/narration-ideas.

Book of Centuries

A Book of Centuries is like a timeline in a notebook. As its name suggests, each two-page spread in the book is devoted to one hundred years—a century—of history. Each student creates his or her own book, recording historical events and names of importance, along with pictures, poems, quotes, and anything else that makes the book individual. You can also add written narrations, illustrations from the Internet, or titles of books you've read that are set in that time period. As they add more history to the book, the students begin to make relations between people who lived in the same era.

Books of Centuries can be as simple or elaborate as you desire. If you want a simple one, download a free Book of Centuries template at http://simplycm.com/BOC.

We recommend each student in grades 7–12 create his own Book of Centuries. If your students are not yet old enough to take on the responsibility of their own Books of Centuries, you could create one together as a family.

Watch for helpful dates in the timeline column throughout the lessons in this book. You don't have to add every event listed; feel free to pick and choose. Dates are taken from *All Through the Ages,* revised second edition. If you are using a reference book that presents alternate dates, feel free to use those instead in your Book of Centuries. The purpose of this book is not to defend or refute certain dating, but to try to place Bible events in the broad context of world events. (Note: A "c" beside a date stands for "circa," which means "about" or "approximately.")

A Word on Mythology

When studying Ancient History, you will inevitably encounter mythology. Be careful about allowing young children to fill their minds with stories about false gods and goddesses. They need to know that these people who lived in ancient times worshiped false gods and invented stories about them, but they do not need to spend large amounts of time studying those false gods and learning every detail about those stories. Instead, make sure your children have a firm foundation in the truth about the one true God and interpret mythology through what Scripture says about it.

We often refer to Romans 1:20–25 when studying mythology. God's power, attributes (characteristics), and divine nature (the fact that He is the one true God) are clearly seen in His creation. The ancients saw His handiwork but they chose not to honor Him or give Him thanks. Instead, they chose to turn their worship to gods in the form of men and beasts (v. 23). They exchanged the truth of God for a lie and worshiped and served things that He created rather than the Creator Himself (v. 25).

Usually, I explain mythology something like this: "Myths are pretend stories these people made up instead of believing in God. Reading them can give us a good peek inside these people's hearts, because they often imagined their gods to be the same way they were themselves (moody, revengeful, selfish, etc.). Just keep in mind that the stories are pretend."

If you are following the Simply Charlotte Mason Curriculum Guide's suggestions for History and Bible, your child will have a good foundation in Scripture and truth before he is exposed to Greek and Roman mythology. Older children can learn more about mythology details than younger children, but still beware of how much mythology they are filling their minds with. I try to make sure that the children are getting as much (or more!) Bible into their minds as they are getting myths inside them during these Ancient History studies.

Suggestions toward Calculating Credits

Keeping track of high school credits is always a challenge but not that hard once you get the hang of it. You can calculate the credits based on actual time spent interacting with the material, or you can calculate credits based on the amount of work involved. Most authorities agree that if you are calculating based on actual time spent, a credit is awarded for every 120–180 hours spent on task, with 150 being average.

For the completion of grades 7–9 or 10–12 assignments in this Joshua through Malachi & Ancient Greece study, I suggest that students should be awarded ½ credit for History/Geography, plus ½ credit for Bible. Usually Geography is included with History and considered one course of study. It is up to you whether you want to consider Bible as a separate course or include it as part of History, since the focus is on Israel's history in ancient times. If you want to combine History, Geography, and Bible, award 180 hours, or 1 full History credit.

Below are details demonstrating how the credit suggestions for this study were calculated. The calculations for Hours Spent are an estimated average. The calculations below for the Course Work Detail assume the student completed all the readings and assignments given in these lesson plans for grades 7–9 or 10–12.

Hours Spent

History & Geography—½ Credit
Average 2.5 hours per week x 36 weeks = 90 hours

Bible—½ Credit
Average 2.5 hours per week x 36 weeks = 90 hours

Course Work Detail

History

Grades 7–9
847 pages read in 5 books
36 written narrations
16 artifacts studied
Book of Centuries project
3 essay exams

Grades 10–12
1167 pages read in 5 books
46 written narrations
16 artifacts studied
Book of Centuries project
3 essay exams

Geography

Grades 7–12
29 map studies and drills
137 pages read in 2 books
31 integrated map work in History and Bible lessons

Bible

Grades 7–12
450 pages read in 1 book
(more if the optional corresponding psalms and entire prophetic books were read)
6–8 written narrations
8-month Proverbs Bible study project
Discovering Doctrine project
3 essay exams